10/23/11

For BJ —
Thank you for
your support —
Be happy and
healthy in love!
Jill

# Confessions of a Love Addict

Jill Williams

*Jill Williams*

D1475586

Aberdeen Bay

Harbin - San Diego - Washington, D. C.

Aberdeen Bay
Published by Aberdeen Bay, an imprint of Champion Writers.
www. aberdeenbay. com

International Standard Book Number
ISBN-13: 978-1-60830-059-4
ISBN-10: 1-60830-059-5

Printed in the United States of America.

*For Leon Haller*
*who never got to read this*

# Acknowledgments

To all the people who have helped me along the way. Your willing ears and useful comments have made this a much better book. If I have left your name out, please forgive the omission. A debt of gratitude goes to, in no particular order: Bonnie Meyer, Marg Nelson, Ted Schrader, Robin McClure, Wally Brown, Penny Gummerson, Sally Emmerson, Carl Weis, Lorie Pomeroy, Jack Deshida, Kathleen Nering, Sharon Cooke, Ken Rouse, Will Burkhart, Lance Eastman, Sue Clemenz, Ed Kessler, Carol Croland, Terry Tyner, John Carr, Benni Heacock.

# LOVE GHOST

As unexpected as an early frost,
Or someone dying in a hit-and-run,
His presence in my life is never lost,
Despite the months of self-inflicted fun.
Like weeds, some loves will never go away.
They may lie dormant, hiding underground.
But give it time and suddenly one day
They sprout again and spin your world around.
"Not me," I say, "I've done that dance before.
"I wish him well but not in my embrace."
How strong I sound – like surf against the shore,
Such raw determination on my face.
But then the phone line flickers, soft and dim,
And damned if I'm not praying that it's him. . . .

- Jill Williams -

# PROLOGUE

## In the beginning

### December 31

It's New Year's Eve. I'm spending it with my stepson and his perky little girlfriend. They've come down from Canada to visit me in Sedona, Arizona. We've had a pleasant couple of days, done a little hiking, played Charades. Nobody dares mention his dad. They think it will upset me; I think it will make them feel uncomfortable. So here we are, pretending my ex doesn't exist. Nine months ago his son begged me in tears to go over to his dad's place. Convinced his pop was dying, he didn't want him to be alone. He also knew I had the power to change all that. Of course, he wasn't willing to go there himself. Who wants to surprise a drunk in the middle of committing suicide?

### Nine Months Earlier

I'd returned to Vancouver for the summer and when my ex opened the door, I was horrified. His rail-thin legs could no longer support him as he gripped the doorknob in desperation. And his Delta blues voice had turned old man shaky. He was even more shocked to see me standing there. He must have assumed I was still back in the states. We lessened the tension with some light banter, acting as if nothing about my surprise visit was unusual. He read me passages from the book he'd been working on about his rebellious youth, growing up in Florida. We'd originally met in a creative writing class. I was the teacher, he was a student. Talented, charming and extremely handsome, he invited me out to dinner several months after the class had ended to critique the final draft of his short story. The chemistry was instant. Within days, we were sharing the same bed. Listening to him read what he'd written now was heart-breaking. The mindless ramblings of a full-blown alcoholic. But I knew, by doing this, I would regain his trust. He promised to see our family physician the next day. To make sure he went, I offered him a ride. The doctor prescribed hundreds of dollar's worth of pills for gout, acid reflux, depression, insomnia. All booze-related illnesses. As we waited for the pharmacist to fill his order, I suggested we go to a nearby café, hoping he'd eat something. The most he could swallow was two mini-bites of a bran muffin. How could this hero of mine—someone I had loved so loyally for so many years—let himself spiral this much out of control? We parted after a sexless hug. For the next week, he sent me a barrage of emails begging me to take him back. He wanted us to be a couple again but he wasn't quite ready to quit drinking. Well, I wasn't quite ready to live with an active alcoholic.

### Back to the Present

I'm trying to stay awake so I can wish my house guests a "Happy 2008!" It's not easy. One of the disconcerting signs of aging is that bedtime keeps getting earlier. In a last ditch effort to prevent my eyelids from shutting before midnight, I walk over to my laptop. Has anyone wished me a Happy New Year? There it is, taunting me like a pea-sized lump I discover on my breast while showering. An email from my ex saying he's been sober three months and wants to try, one last time, to see if we can have a healthy, loving relationship. Shit. I don't know what to do. I should delete it. Immediately. Instead, I reread his words, savoring them like some food I'm allergic to but can't resist. We begin corresponding. Two, maybe three times a week. His words ring truer. He seems more grounded. As always, his humor is unerringly seductive. We flirt. We fantasize. And pretty soon I'm telling myself, "This time will be different."

# PART ONE – HOPE

Hope is the thing with feathers
that perches in the soul and
sings the tune without the words
and never stops at all.

- Emily Dickinson -

# CHAPTER ONE

## Why go back again?

After three months of sobriety, my ex wants to try again. Open to the idea, I'm like a soldier entering enemy territory wary of emotional land mines. We've broken up and ricocheted back together more times than I care to remember. But I do remember. Seven breakups, seven reunions, over a period of fifteen years. When we first met, I was in my late forties. Now I pay senior prices for movie tickets. It would be so nice if we could finally get it right this time.

Still, I'm scared. Do I risk making yet another self-destructive decision?

I'm crazy about the man. He makes me laugh. He stimulates my mind. He's the protective dad I never had, the playful brother I always wanted, the lover who thinks I'm the most desirable woman on the planet. He's also an egotistical bastard who is far more comfortable making up stories than telling the truth.

I want to believe he's changed. I want to believe I've changed, too. In fact, I know I have. We first met in Canada, where I used to live. Now, I'm a transplanted Arizonan. If this eighth attempt at reconciliation were to succeed, I would never move back there. It's too cold, too damp, and those endless winters are too damn depressing.

I was doing fine before his email arrived. I'd made new friends, built a reasonably happy life for myself. I'm reminded of a Joshua Kadison lyric about a guy who loves a girl named Jessie. She calls him from a phone booth in Vegas, asking him to join her and her cat Moses on a trip to Mexico. His response is very much the way I'm feeling right now: "*Oh, Jessie, you always do this every time I get back on my feet.*"

I've decided to give my sometimes-partner a pseudonym. He's typical of his astrology sign. Proud, playful, thinks the world revolves around him. So from now on my former lover, ex husband and full blown addiction shall be known as Leo. Part of me wants to get back together. Another part feels I'd be making a serious mistake. Maybe, if I force myself to remember why the relationship never lasts, I'll come to my senses before it's too late.

### New York City – 1997

It's fall. The air is as crisp as a Granny Smith apple and we're in the middle of Times Square on holiday. I've known Leo a year now. We've recently purchased a townhouse together and are hard at work coauthoring a screenplay. Leo has a serious drinking problem. I've got an equally serious one trying to control his booze intake. I also want to prove that I'm not an alcoholic. As an example, I'll buy us each our own bottle of Cabernet Sauvignon. After dinner, I meticulously mark off how much wine is left in my bottle with Liquid Paper Correction Fluid. I have this odd notion that if someone doesn't finish an entire bottle of wine, they aren't an alcoholic. Leo always finishes his and then proceeds to polish off the rest of mine.

So here we are, walking down Broadway, soaking up the sights. Lindy's, the Camel cigarette sign puffing out smoke, "Evita." I bump into an old friend. He and his wife join us for dinner and we all get pretty schnockered. After waving a dozen inebriated goodbyes, Leo and I stagger back to the West Side apartment where we're staying. We sing, we giggle. We try unsuccessfully to avoid stepping on sidewalk cracks. One thing about drunks, their moods can change in an instant. We buy some coffee from a surly clerk and suddenly we start picking on each other. "Honey" becomes "Bitch!" "Cutie" becomes "Prick!" By the time we get inside the apartment, any semblance of self-control has vanished.

I punch him in the chest, he pushes me away. I try kicking him in his privates, he pushes me harder. Before we know what's happened, I can't feel anything in my left arm. The upper half is completely disconnected from the lower half. Leo's final push has knocked me to the ground. Suddenly we're both very sober. Phoning the nearest emergency room,

I find out what it will cost without medical insurance. The thrifty New Englander in me rebels. I decide to tough it out until the following morning when we're scheduled to fly back to Canada where I do have medical insurance.

We play "Hangman" on the flight home, my left arm wrapped tightly in a makeshift sling. Leo acts contrite. He's unusually quiet. I don't have a clue what he's thinking. Me, I just want to find out how bad the injury is. After he collects our luggage, we take a cab to the nearest hospital. According to the X-rays, my left arm has sustained a bad break. The nurse studies me a little too carefully as I try to explain how I tripped on a rug and fell. She doesn't believe a word I'm saying.

For the next six weeks, Leo is my caregiver. We go into therapy where anger management classes are strongly recommended. Leo attends these hour long sessions every Monday night, grateful to me for not pressing charges.

Even so, we both agree our relationship is over.

I still feel a certain shame about that fight. How could someone with my advantages—a good education, decent upbringing, lots of friends—put herself in a situation where her arm gets broken by the man who supposedly loves her? "It was the alcohol," I tell myself. "We were both incredibly drunk."

**A Year Later**

Like so many other couples who can't end relationships, we couldn't either. Within nine months Leo and I boomeranged back together, confident that marriage was the missing ingredient. Our wedding—a second for both of us—took place eight days before Christmas. Continuing to drink alcoholically, we rationalized our behavior by denying it. We'd fight verbally but never again got physical with each other. The condo we lived in was on the sixteenth floor, overlooking downtown Vancouver. Leo's office was in the bedroom; we slept in the living room. I can still picture that pullout couch with its roughly woven fabric of lavender, pale blue and pink. Lumpy as hell, the oak armrests gave it a touch of class.

This particular night, like most nights, we'd had plenty

to drink. When I opened my eyes the next morning and saw an empty condom wrapper on the coffee table, I squinted up at Leo and asked, "What's that? "

"You don't remember, do you."

"I do, too!" I replied, defensively.

He led me into the bathroom and when I saw my neck covered in hickeys, something I don't normally tolerate, I was speechless. Obviously, I'd been in a blackout during our love-making. For a woman who prides herself on being in complete control at all times, this was unnerving.

It shook Leo up, too.

When he went to his psychiatrist, a man he'd been seeing for over a year, he told him about my blacking out. The good doctor suggested we give up booze for a month. If we weren't able to, we'd know we had a serious drinking problem. I was incensed. My husband was the alcoholic, not me. Still, I was scared enough to attend an AA meeting. Then another. And another. Thankfully I heard what I needed to hear and haven't picked up a drink since. Leo's journey has been far more circuitous. Trying to quit any addiction as a newlywed couple is a bitch. For us, it was the kiss of divorce.

### Early Spring - 2002

After our divorce, Leo moved to another section of the city. Months went by without any contact but eventually the boomerang effect kicked in. We rented an apartment together in Kitsilano, a residential area inhabited mostly by students attending the University of British Columbia.

It was our third attempt at "blissful domesticity."

By now, I have five consecutive years of sobriety, Leo has nine months. He's been in and out of AA and has finally accepted the fact that, as an alcoholic, he can never pick up another drink. He seems genuinely committed to his recovery this time. To be on the safe side, we meet weekly with a couples' counselor. Barry, a recovering alcoholic himself, looks like a roly-poly version of Ernest Hemingway—an author Leo has worshiped and tried to emulate his entire life.

He begins complaining about his lack of energy, fitful sleep patterns. He can't seem to get motivated. Because his mom suffered from depression, Leo takes a little yellow and green Prozac pill every morning to ward off his own dark tendencies. Based on these symptoms, Barry urges him to ask his medical doctor to increase the dosage.

"I may just do that," he says without much enthusiasm.

Later that day, a girlfriend of mine from Winnipeg arrives. She's staying with us for a week. Next morning as we're sipping our first cup of steaming caffeine, Leo waves goodbye. He's off to Starbucks to meet with his AA sponsor, something he does every Friday morning at eight o'clock. I'm so proud of him. Like a lot of men, he has a hard time reaching out to other men for help.

"How'd the session go?" I ask, as we're getting ready for bed that evening.

"It was intense. We got into some heavy shit."

"That's good!" I'm relieved, knowing how crucial this is for any alcoholic's recovery.

"I think I'm making real progress this time."

"I know you are," I tell him, overcome with a sense of gratitude.

When I wake up, I always check my emails. This particular morning, I see an email from Leo's sponsor. He must have sent it to my address by mistake. Apologizing for missing yesterday's session, he wants to know when Leo would like to make it up. I don't want my poor houseguest to witness the screaming match I know is about to take place, so I—very calmly, very sweetly—suggest that he and I go for a stroll around the block. He likes the idea.

Once outside, my accusations fly at him like a swarm of angry bees. "Why did you lie to me about seeing your sponsor yesterday?"

He says nothing.

"What have I ever done to you to deserve such total disrespect?"

More silence.

"You promised me you'd never lie to me again!"

"So, I'm a liar." His eyes blaze with fury. "You want *more* truth? You know those Prozac pills you're always bugging me to take? Well, I just pretend to be taking them along with my vitamins. You may want me to be your pussy-

whipped little boy but it'll never happen!"
    I was stunned. His former psychiatrist had prescribed
Prozac to help Leo with his mood swings. I had nothing to do
with it. He packed his bags and moved out within hours.

                                    . . .

    You'd think I'd want nothing more to do with this
man. But you'd be wrong. As a love addict, I refuse to accept
the idea that sometimes enough is enough. Instead, I become
preoccupied — no, obsessed — with saving relationships.

    The first question I need to ask myself is:

*Why go back again?*

    When I was a little girl, my mother would come
into my bedroom and tuck me under the covers. "G'nite,
Mommy!" I'd squeal. "See you in the morning!"
    "You never can tell," she'd reply.
    As an adult I assume she was just being ironic. Back
then, I was afraid I'd never see her again. This has indelibly
shaped the way I view love relationships. Will everyone
eventually leave me? My mother's nighttime sign off made me
feel abandoned, discarded, forgotten. "Better to love someone
than no one," I keep telling myself. Or, "Better the devil you
know than the devil you don't."
    I may not be the poster child for mental health but the
first step toward getting there is recognizing why I feel the
way I do. What Mommy used to tell me every night doesn't
have to dictate who I am today. Or who I fall in love with.

# CHAPTER TWO

## Is being alone that bad?

"Anything worth doing is worth overdoing." That's the advice my insurance-selling dad would offer his fellow agents every time a sales pitch got turned down. His oft-repeated phrase epitomizes the way I used to live my life—and still do, in some areas. Whenever Leo and I would call it quits, I'd return to those online dating sites with the dedication of an athlete in training for a marathon.

I'm a petite woman with a good figure, which made finding potential mates easier. I'm also funny and a bit outrageous. Here's a list of adjectives I put in my profile: Slim, silly, enthusiastic, financially independent, creative, eccentric. I could write an entire book on my internet dating experiences. For me, making romantic connections online has always been a piece of cake.

Sometimes that cake is delicious.

Other times, it's inedible.

My choices, like most love addicts, have been less than stellar. In each case, I'd convince myself that whoever I was dating would make me feel whole again. Unfortunately, the euphoria never lasted.

### Carson - 1998

After the fight Leo and I had in New York City, I immediately got on Match. com and found Carson. He couldn't have been more different than Leo. Balding, wiry, high-pitched voice. Still, he had these mesmerizing steel blue eyes. (Leo's were brown.) We met for lunch in a French restaurant. One look at those eyes and I knew exactly what I wanted to do. Make mad, passionate love on the bed I'd been sharing with Leo for the past nine months.

There's nothing quite as satisfying as revenge sex.
Naturally, Carson had problems. His ex wife kept
begging him to take her back. And he had this blind cat, Zoey,
who refused to eat unless he kept there hand-feeding her. He
was also preoccupied with his prize-winning daffodils. They
were far more important to him than any woman.

We didn't work out. He was too involved with his ex,
I was too involved with mine. Much later, Leo confessed that
he'd gotten hold of Carson's phone number, called him up and
threatened to "hurt him" if he didn't leave me alone. I never
checked the story out with Carson. Who needs to catch Leo in
yet another lie?

### Gary - 1999

Two things I remember about Gary. Whenever I asked
him any personal questions — where he grew up, where he
went to school, what his current occupation was — he'd cry,
"Probe alert! Probe alert!" Funny at first, the routine got old
after awhile. Then there was this huge, flapjack of a birthmark
on Gary's back. When we first had sex, I tried not to notice
it. Which only made me notice it more. We met at one of
those singles dinners where the conversation is often stilted
and insincere. Gary was off in a corner getting pleasantly
plastered. Once we dispensed with the social chitchat, I found
him extremely well-educated and witty. In the middle of
writing a musical for The Vancouver Fringe Festival, I was
dumbfounded when Gary offered to pay the three hundred
dollar entrance fee. Drunk or not, it was a very generous
gesture.

Our second date was a disaster. He literally drank
himself under the table. I left him there at the restaurant and
walked home by myself. Next day, he was profusely apologetic.
I told him it was okay, everybody screws up once in awhile.
Still, trading one booze hound for another didn't make much
sense. Like geraniums in the sun, my romance with Gary faded
fast. Nonetheless, I invited him to the cast party.

I also invited Leo.

### Robin – Summer of 2002

I received an email from a fan in Switzerland. The guy had read some of my poetry online and wanted to congratulate me. Unlike most of today's slam poets, I use classical forms like sonnets and villanelles to express myself. Robin (that was his name) began corresponding with me. I soon learned that he was around my age, Oxford-educated and a definite "silver fox." Growing up in Cambridge, England, he now lived in Geneva. The more we emailed back and forth, the clearer it became that Robin was smitten. So much so, that he insisted on flying halfway across the globe to meet me.

To make our first intimate encounter less performance-pressured and more fun, he wore a Batman cape and painted a happy face on his penis. It broke the ice, all right. And the gift he brought me made us laugh even harder. In one of my sillier emails, I'd confessed that I'd always wanted my very own appendage so I could pee my name in the snow. After he'd unpacked, and we were enjoying a spot of Earl Grey tea, Robin presented me with a skin-colored ceramic mug that had an unusual-looking spout. On it, he'd inscribed:

> *Dear wonderful goddess, please know*
> *I adore and I worship you so*
> *I hope that this gift*
> *Will give you a lift*
> *For now you can write in the snow!*

Robin had problems too. He'd been a successful engineer for Motorola but after 9/11 his job had ceased to exist. Now he worked at a recycling plant, sorting garbage on a conveyor belt, which is undoubtedly where he'd spied the penis-mug. Aside from being poor, Robin was heavily into Scientology. He tried not to proselytize but a fanatic is a fanatic no matter what his beliefs are. Robin was also married, claiming it was a "marriage-of-convenience" (for immigration purposes only). I soon learned that his young Moroccan wife was three months pregnant by her boss. As far as the Swiss government was concerned, she and her offspring

were Robin's financial responsibility regardless of who the
father was. Even for a chaos junkie like me, this was too much
baggage to handle.

...

Hard as I've tried to replace Leo with a new man, it
never works. Dr. Daniel Amen has been doing brain scans
and says that the one we love actually occupies space in the
brain and, when we lose that relationship, our brain continues
to look for our loved one. For awhile I'll fool myself into
believing I don't need Leo. Then an old Mose Allison tune will
come on the radio. Or I'll hear someone with a deeply male
voice. And my craving takes over. I call it a temporary longing
rather than an obsession. Sort of like a chocoholic who tells
herself it's the last Hershey bar she'll ever buy.

According to sex therapist Karen K. Harrison, "Taking
some time between relationships to process our grief, and
learn from the relationship before moving on, makes it more
likely that the next relationship will be healthy."

I've tried it both ways. When I'm with someone else,
I end up resenting him for not being Leo. If I'm alone, I get
paralyzed with fear that no one will ever love me again. Funny
how I say love *me* again, rather than finding someone *I* can
love. Am I capable of love? Who knows.

*Is being alone that bad?*

My friends used to laugh when I'd tell them, "I can't
bear the thought that someday I'll die sitting on the john and
Joe, the building manager, will be the first one to discover
the body!" Of course, Joe has since died and I've moved to a
different part of the country. Still, the fear of dying alone is
fairly universal. For me, an even bigger fear is being without
a partner. I love sharing. A good meal, a rousing game of gin
rummy. If I had to create a t-shirt slogan that summarized my
philosophy, it would read, "Bonding Is Better!"

Alas, too many Carsons, Garys and Robins have
lessened this need of mine for constant companionship. Until
Leo's email arrived, I'd convinced myself that being alone

for the rest of my life wouldn't be so bad. I could do my own thing, be my own boss. Now that he's back, I'm terrified I might lose him again. When we're in bed, intertwined like morning glories, I feel safe and protected. Knowing he'll be there the next morning to share a coffee gives me a natural high. Even his smell is somehow comforting. Can I help it if my breath catches every time he sneaks up behind me and starts nibbling at the nape of my neck?

# CHAPTER THREE

## What are my expectations?

### ONE LAST TIME

She sits outside, her freckles multiplying.
And thinks of him and feels a certain heat.
The sun, of course! That's why her skin is frying
And why soft beads of sweat caress her feet.
It's not about the odds they're both defying,
The trying, one last time, to be complete.
It's just the sun, of course! (Poor girl, she's lying.
Her innocence, like jasmine, smells so sweet.)
They've vowed to take it slower, tread with care.
They've sworn they'll make reality a friend.
She fans her face in need of cooler air,
Determined not to think how it might end.
How often do our former dreams survive?
That's not the point. It's hope that makes love thrive.

- Jill Williams -

Ever since Leo asked me to give our relationship another try, I've been cautiously optimistic. When he first contacted me, he requested that we limit our communication to emails only. He maintained that once he heard my voice, he wouldn't be able to be objective. I went along with this because I knew he was right. I also wanted him to feel he was in complete control of when and how we reunited. For the next three months we emailed back and forth, sharing our hopes and fears about a potential future together. Would he continue lying to me when the truth was inconvenient? Would I continue micromanaging his every move? At the exact same moment, we sent each other the identical email:" I think it's

time for us to meet in person." His son suggested we pick
a town neither of us had ever been to, some place new and
unexplored. Like the relationship we were about to embark
on.

## Reunion In Tucson - 2009

Nothing compares to spring in the desert. Golden
Barrel, Capitol Reef, Hedgehog cacti are in full bloom,
brightening the normally dull brown earth with colorful
insistence. The giant saguaro (pronounced "sa-WAH-ro") look
like prickly pickles on steroids. Despite the city's confusing
street patterns, it's an ideal place for lovers to reunite. I was
nervous driving down to the airport. It had been two years
since we'd seen each other. Would Leo still want me? My long
but graying hair, my less than youthful breasts?
      When we first saw each other, neither of us knew
what to say. He just stared at me in disbelief. Was this really
happening? I was driving so I couldn't stare back. His deeply
masculine voice made me quiver inside. The intense love we'd
always felt hadn't changed. But other things had.
      Leo didn't bug me about my driving, I didn't bug him
about his dyed beard. He didn't put down my country music
station, I didn't put down his clothing choices. Throughout
the week we behaved differently. If any little thing went
wrong — TV not working, noisy kids in the hot tub, getting lost
in a strange city — we took it in stride. There was no tension
whatsoever.
      These seven days weren't meant to seal our fate. We
just wanted to have fun, act like teenagers. As always, the
sexual vibes were electric. We'd agreed beforehand to keep
this initial meeting cuddly, not coital. Once intimacy was
involved, objectivity became a thing of the past. Even without
sex, Leo and I couldn't keep our hands off one another. It felt
wonderful to be a couple again. But how long, I wondered,
would "wonderful" last? I'm reminded of a Stephen Sondheim
lyric from "Company:"

> *It's sharing little winks together,*
> *Drinks together,*

*Kinks together,*
*That make marriage a joy.*
*It's bargains that you shop together,*
*Cigarettes you stop together,*
*Clothing that you swap together,*
*That makes perfect relationships.*
*[3 verses later]*
*It's people that you hate together,*
*Bait together,*
*Date together,*
*That make marriage a joy.*
*It's things like using force together,*
*Shouting till you're hoarse together,*
*Getting a divorce together,*
*That make perfect relationships.**

I wasn't expecting a perfect relationship. Still, our week together in Tucson gave me hope that a workable one was entirely possible. After Leo boarded the plane back to Canada, my careful optimism blossomed into a firm conviction that this reunion had the makings of forever.

### Summer In Sedona - 2009

Leo arrived in mid-July for another month long visit. Summer is normally monsoon season but, like our newly developing relationship, there wasn't a single storm cloud during his entire visit. In looking over my calendar notations, we kept ourselves busy. Hiking, attending a writers' workshop, going to an Indian reservation to help a friend build a *hogan* (a traditional Navajo home). Leo went to several AA meetings while he was here and that felt good, too. His sharing seemed more genuine. He didn't try to impress anybody or deflect what he was really feeling with humor.

* LITTLE THINGS YOU DO TOGETHER Written by Stephen Sondheim
Used by permission of Herald Square Music, Inc. On behalf of Range Road
Music, Inc., Jerry Leiber Music, Silver Seahorse Music LLC and
Rilting Music, Inc.

Even when we were off doing our own thing, that felt easy and natural. There continued to be absolutely no friction between us. Just love. Laughter. And the sound of our racing hearts.

We'd gotten into the rhythm of living together — deciding where to eat, which trail to explore, when to read aloud to each another. We both enjoyed that tremendously. Driving Leo to the airport, I tried to hide how badly I felt. Waving goodbye from my car, I made a silly face so he wouldn't sense my sadness. On the way back to Sedona, I forced myself to focus on the next time we'd be together. Only six weeks away. Still the idea of returning to that empty condo, sharing meals with a memory, was something I wasn't looking forward to. That's the thing about loving someone. When they're gone it feels like they're still there. Until it hits you that they aren't. Probably the same way an amputee feels about a missing limb.

### Six Weeks Later

It was my turn to visit Leo. The apartment he currently owned and occupied was in the West End of Vancouver, overlooking English Bay. As always, his bedroom served as his business office. By now we were getting serious about when Leo might move to Sedona permanently. No dates had been mentioned and I didn't push it. I'd learned from past experience that pressuring Leo was an exercise in futility.

Under most circumstances my style is to blunder ahead with blinders on, whereas Leo likes to examine, re-examine and re-re-examine all sides to any problem before making a decision. Our wildly differing approaches had often caused major blow-ups. Not anymore. Diplomacy was the name of the game now, compromise its companion.

I'm deeply touched by the little things Leo has done in anticipation of my arrival. It's a small apartment but he's managed to stuff all his belongings into the bedroom closet so the one in the hall is empty — and waiting for me. Entering his bathroom, I see that he's also cleared out a drawer for my cosmetics. Considering there are only two drawers in that tiny bathroom, I'm impressed. He's even bought me my own china teacup. (I prefer them to mugs.) These gestures make me feel welcome, wanted and even a little bit worshipped.

On the rare evenings when we eat at home and the main meal is over, I bring our desserts in from the kitchen and place them on his dining room table. Whether it's carrot cake or blueberry lemon squares, by the time I get back with two cups of freshly brewed coffee, my plate is missing.

"Hey, where's my dessert?" I act shocked.

"Dessert? What dessert? " He feigns total innocence.

During my return to the kitchen, he's hidden my dessert. It's a ritual we've perfected over the years. To some it may seem childish. To me, Leo's playfulness is one his most endearing qualities. Another is his insistence that he give me a twenty-minute back rub every morning. Who could resist such a delicious offer?

. . .

When it comes to expectations, I'm reminded of a definition I heard at an AA meeting: "*Expectations are resentments in the making.*" I try very hard not to let my expectations get the better of me. The best way to do that is by expressing any hopes I have up front. If they're realistic, great. If they aren't? So be it. Unspoken assumptions are relationship killers. Leo and I used to assume all over the place and it invariably caused misunderstandings and heartache. Now, if I have an opinion about what I think our long term goals should be, I verbalize it. No more secrets, no more second-guessing.

*What are my expectations?*

Sobriety. Respect. Honesty.

Am I being unrealistic here?

A few years ago, after I'd been complaining bitterly about Leo's inability to tell the truth, my sponsor suggested I write down the following affirmation: "My lover lies. I choose to be with him. And that's okay." Eager to do anything she advised, I wrote:

My lover lies. (Yes, that's true.)

I choose to be with him. (That's true, too.)

And that's okay. (Hey, wait a sec! That's not okay.)

Her point was that I had chosen to be with Leo. It was my choice and I could just as easily choose to leave him if he continued lying.

I did leave him that time. I just couldn't handle any more of his unwarranted "embellishments."

Leo gets that now.

Day after day, phone call after phone call, I see his determination to be rigorously honest. Even if it means disappointing me or making me angry. The more truthful he is, the easier it is on both of us. As a byproduct of this new behavior, I've become less controlling. Leo covets his freedom. He needs time and space to write his short stories, play guitar, study the night sky uninterrupted. These days, I respect that need much more than I ever used to.

# CHAPTER FOUR

## How important is sex?

Sex used to be a big bone of contention (pardon the pun) between us. Leo has always been more into it than I have. Despite the many hours we'd spend pleasuring each other — kissing, caressing, climaxing — I always felt he was disappointed that my passion quota never quite equaled his.

Gender differences between the sexes have been written about for centuries. Our brain sizes are not the same, language skills, the way men and women approach and solve problems. One of the biggest differences is how we feel about sex. The classic clichés tend to make women crave an emotional connection, whereas men just want to get off.

Romantic words don't do it for me. My first husband Joel used to set the stage by lighting candles, putting soft music on in the background. Me, I was more of a wham-bam-thank-you-ma'am type.

When Leo first discovered this sexual predilection of mine, he remarked, "Why didn't I know you back in high school? " He went on to explain that when he was a teenager, he'd focus his mind on baseball stats so he wouldn't ejaculate prematurely. My need for speed wasn't because I didn't enjoy sex. I did. I just found those declarations of love during foreplay a distraction.

How a man looks, how he performs, is far more stimulating to me than what he says in bed. Don't get me wrong. After sex, I love being held and told how wonderful I am. That's music to the ears of any card-carrying love addict. But when I was younger, sexual situations that involved danger or being unconventional stimulated me more.

### Summer - 1964

I'd just finished my freshman year at Sarah Lawrence College and was taking an art history course in Florence, Italy. The plan was to meet my sister in Paris after the course ended. On my own in Europe at age nineteen, I felt very grown up and independent. Although living in a magical villa with frescoes painted on every wall and four poster beds in every room, my single focus was on Italian men.

Ucchio Pignatelli was introduced to me by one of the other art students. His rugged Jean-Paul Belmondo looks were an immediate turn-on. We toured the city on his red Vespa, crisscrossing the Arno, waving at Michelangelo's "David" in the square, zigzagging along a beautiful road called the Via Chiantigiana. Eventually, he took me to his *appartamento*, we drank lots of *vino rosso* and eventually *facciamo l'amore*. I wasn't a virgin but I wasn't particularly experienced, either. For me it was more "*L'avventura italiana.*'

Summer school ends in two days. Ucchio urges me to skip class and come with him to "the most beautiful beach in all of Italy." While trying not to gawk at the topless sunbathers, I strike up a conversation with another Italian named Antonio. Suddenly, Ucchio grabs my arm and practically drags me off the beach. The ride back to town is tense. When we get to his place, he explains that he has an errand to do but will return shortly. The sound of a key being inserted from the outside and the eventual clicking shut of a lock makes me painfully aware that I'm trapped in this man's apartment.

How long will he keep me here?

I scour the place, searching for a telephone. No luck. There's a window in the bedroom but it won't open. Now I'm beginning to panic. My eyes well up with tears, partly from frustration but mostly out of fear. An hour later, I hear the sound of approaching footsteps and the tumbler turning. When Ucchio enters the apartment, I plead with him to forgive me for even looking at another man, swearing on the cross he's wearing around his neck that my heart belongs to him.

He doesn't believe me.

Maybe seduction will salve his wounded pride.

When I try to kiss him he pushes me away, saying he's too disappointed in me to want to make love. After placing his keys in a jar on the top shelf of a bookcase I could never reach, he undresses and falls easily into bed. As he snores, innocent as an angel, I lie awake beside him—picturing my poor sister waiting for me at Orly Airport.

The next morning, Ucchio leaves bright and early for work. (If memory serves me correctly, he was a postal clerk.) Again, he locks me in. The landlady must have a spare key. Maybe, if I yell loud enough....

Nobody answers.

I bang my fists against the living room wall, hoping a neighbor might come to my rescue.

More silence.

Utterly defeated, I flop down on the bed and fall asleep.

The sound of a key in the lock jolts me awake. My Italian captor has returned home for lunch. He seems a little friendlier so I snuggle up to him, twirling his chest hairs with my index finger. Soon we're huffing and puffing away until Ucchio finally grunts in spent satisfaction, still refusing to let me leave.

He falls asleep with the house key dangling from his pants pocket. I suppose, if I'd really wanted to, I could try and escape at this point. But as terrifying as the situation is, it excites me. When Ucchio wakes up, we have sex again. It's better for both of us this time. I whisper huskily, "You can't keep me here forever, you know." He studies me carefully. "Maybe next time you won't be so free with your words to another man."

When Ucchio leaves for work, I wait to hear the sound of that ancient key turning in the lock. Nothing happens. I wait a minute longer and tentatively try the inside door handle. It opens. In the distance, I hear a Vespa gurgling to life. Whew. Now I'll be able to catch that plane and meet my sister in Paris. I'll give her a big hug but I certainly won't tell her about my last two days in Florence.

### Malibu, California - 1985

As a journalist, I've written plenty of magazine articles. One, in particular comes to mind. It was a two part series where I first asked men, and then women, what their biggest sexual turn on was. With men, I was amazed how many of them put great stock in where they did the deed, not how they did it. I remember one ex cop said his ideal sex fantasy consisted of getting a flatbed truck, putting it in low gear and "doing it" on a blanket in the back, as he and some babe rolled slowly through high desert country under the stars. (I can't think of a more uncomfortable scenario, myself.)

My place fantasy involved doing it directly below The Chart House in Malibu, California. Built on stilts, the restaurant juts out over the beach along the Pacific Ocean. My boyfriend dared me to make it with him underneath the diners. So while they buttered their bread and dove into their shrimp scampi, we dove into something else....

### The Lexington Avenue Armory - 1964

I was living in Manhattan, a rabid feminist before the term had ever been coined. In my twenties, I was stacked but resented any man who openly appreciated my breasts over my brains. I wasn't into the bar scene, didn't dance, hated wearing high heels, stockings and lipstick. Still, I often wondered what it would be like to have sex with a complete stranger.

By no stretch of the imagination am I political. But when John V. Lindsay ran for mayor of New York City, I couldn't resist volunteering for his campaign, hoping I'd get to shake hands with this handsome, well-chiselled WASP. I was assigned to work at the Lexington Avenue Armory. They'd set up voting booths there and my job was to register the individual voters before they entered the booth. Up walks this gorgeous East Indian man. His teeth are blindingly white in contrast to his caramel-colored skin. He's carrying an engineering book; I figure he must be a student at NYU. We smile. I hand him a form to fill out. We smile again, as he hands the form back to me. I wonder what it would be like to have sex with him?

It's my lunch break. I study his address card and take along a spare. He lives two blocks away on Fifth Avenue. My stride quickens as I approach the building. A uniformed doorman waits at the ready. When he opens the door, I breeze right past him. I've already concocted a story to tell the engineering student: I spilled coffee on the original form and need him to fill out a second one. As he lets me inside the apartment, I notice a huge oil painting of a well-known singer hanging on the wall above a baby grand piano. It's a portrait of the woman he lives with — only she's on tour right now. Without a moment's hesitation, I blurt out the real reason for my visit. I want to see what it feels like to make it with a complete stranger.

I don't remember much about the sex. I was too busy thinking, "Am I really doing this?" The wildness of the act was a hundred times more exciting than the act itself. He wanted to see me again, unfortunately, but this wasn't part of my fantasy. How quickly uncomplicated sex becomes complicated.

...

I believe collaborating on a piece of music or writing a screenplay together can be far more intimate, even satisfying, than making love. Why? Because both participants want the same thing, a good end product. With sex the goals can be entirely different. The man may want to spend hours pleasuring his partner, while she'd rather be watching "Survivor."

Does she admit this to him?

Not if she wants the relationship to last.

Sex experts advise women to be open and honest about their sexual needs.

But what if nothing turns them on?

If you are a love addict, that's not something you're willing to share with your mate. Ironic, isn't it? Leo's a natural born liar. While I'm fiercely truthful except when it comes to sex. We've all faked orgasms yet how many of us confess it to our lovers?

*How important is sex?*

For me, sex has lost its magic. I've reached an age where penetration actually hurts. Forget those inviting ads on TV for lubricants that really work. They don't work on me. When Leo began emailing me this time, he swore his sex drive had slowed way down. He wasn't even sure he could get it up anymore. He also said he was back on Prozac which often effects a person's libido. I was relieved. In the past, Leo wanted me to experience sexual pleasure the same way he experienced it. But men and women, are two very different animals. I'm hoping he's telling me the truth about his current sexual needs. It will save us both a lot of frustration and resentment. This may not be what "Cosmo" is peddling but it's my truth — and I won't pretend anymore that it isn't.

# CHAPTER FIVE

## Will money be an issue?

Leo has had his own business for the past thirty-five years. Despite bouts of alcoholic absenteeism, he's made a pretty decent living. On the other hand, I've often teetered on the financial edge—reassured by the fact that someday I'd be inheriting a comfortable income from my father's estate. This knowledge has instilled in me a certain arrogance about money and its importance. Leo used to call me a "trust fund hippy" and try to make me feel guilty about my impending wealth. He'd argue that without a financial cushion, I wouldn't have dared to be so creative. Bull feathers. Artists, no matter whether they're New England rich or redneck poor, will always find a way to express their talent.

Knowing motherhood would hamper my creative freedom, I chose not to have children. I have never regretted that decision as I've encountered many substitute daughters and sons along the way. Leo chose to procreate. (Or at least not to practice safe sex.) Child support costs money and money necessitates earning a living. So his daydreams of being in a band, gigging from town to town, banging a different chick every night, went up in financial smoke.

I didn't receive my inheritance until I was nearly sixty which meant I had to earn a living, too. To support my artistic existence, I did all sorts of things. Taught creative writing, became a drug counselor, a professional house painter, a medical historian. It got so bad at one point, I was forced to rent out my bedroom and sleep on the living room sofa for six months.

That's all behind me now.

I'm financially secure, medically insured and ready to enjoy however many years I have left. Hopefully with Leo. Henrik Ibsen once wrote, "*Money may be the husk of many things but not the kernel. It brings you food, but not appetite; medicine, but not health; acquaintance, but not friends; servants, but not loyalty; days of joy, but not peace or happiness."*

I couldn't have said it better myself.

### August - 1998

We'd been married eleven months. Leo loves to remind me that, if we'd only lasted a year, we would've been entitled to a free meal at the posh restaurant where our wedding took place. By that time, the friction between us wasn't worth a free anything.

Leo did not want to divorce. He felt we would work things out. I was convinced we couldn't. He was sober but, if anything, that made him harder to live with. His sudden verbal outbursts were both threatening and toxic to the relationship. He claimed he had an addictive personality and, whether it was booze or blues, it would take time to change. On the surface, that made perfect sense. The problem was, by lumping all his addictions together, he didn't fully address his alcoholism. Yes, he attended AA meetings but he never took the program seriously. As a result, he was in a constant state of smoldering sobriety.

I remember this one time we were in a video store, trying to decide which film we wanted to rent. Leo suddenly got so enraged about something—probably my movie preferences—that we wound up screaming at each other until the clerk had to ask us to leave. I had assumed life would get easier once Leo wasn't drinking. If anything, it got a whole lot worse.

The day we met at the lawyer's office to sign the final papers, I didn't have two sticks to rub together. More specifically, two hundred dollars to pay my share of the legal costs. Beet red with embarrassment, I apologized to the lawyer and promised to mail him a check ASAP. Out of the corner of my eye, I noticed my soon-to-be ex scribbling something. He slid a piece of paper over to me across the table and said gruffly, "Here." It was a check for two hundred dollars. If the situation had been reversed, I'm not sure I would've been as charitable.

### Wimbledon - 2001

Our endings were never permanent. On this fourth reconciliation attempt (or was it our fifth?), we'd been back on the love train for three months. My dad had finally expired, leaving me with a sizable inheritance. Not quite ready to act rich, I refused to amend my bag lady lifestyle by driving a decade-old Toyota, shopping at secondhand stores, never getting my nails painted. However, as an avid tennis fan, I did make one exception—centre court tickets for Leo and me to attend The All England Lawn Tennis and Croquet Club, otherwise known as Wimbledon. Bought online from some Scottsdale scalper, they cost me ten thousand dollars.

Leo has never been to Europe. Once again wrestling with sobriety, he's managed to accumulate four booze-free months. But he's nervous as a cat and twice as hissy. When we arrive in London, he bitches about everything. How the Brits put ice in their orange juice, how the toast is always served cold, how pricy everything is. Our hotel room is located directly across the street from a nightclub so revelers keep us awake until the early morning hours when garbage trucks take their place. We do all the touristy things. Ride double-decker buses, try to make the guards outside Buckingham Palace crack a smile, feed the pigeons in Trafalgar Square. Still, you can cut the tension between us with a Robbe & Berking sterling silver butter knife.

Only three more days until Championship Sunday. That's when Leo and I will get to experience some live tennis matches instead of watching them on the tiny, black-and-white television in our noisy hotel room. Unfortunately, for only the third time in a hundred and twenty-three years, it rained on and off for that whole bloody weekend. When you buy tickets for Wimbledon, you buy seats for a specific day. No refunds, no exchanges. So those Sunday center court tickets were useless. Had I purchased insurance for a mere thousand dollars and had it rained continuously for forty-five minutes, I would have been reimbursed.

I took it in stride. After all, I'd bought them with inherited money. Money I secretly felt I had no business having. And if the rain gods chose to deluge the courts that

day, so be it. We could always watch Monday's final (between
Patrick Rafter and Goran Ivanesovic) from some London pub
with a big screen TV.

Leo, on the other hand, was devastated.

Trying to minimize the situation, I remarked, "It's
only money." The minute those three words escaped my lips,
I knew I'd made a mistake. He interpreted them to mean that
my cavalier attitude toward money would never jibe with his
blue collar income. He's a proud Southerner, unaccustomed to
letting a woman treat him to anything. While we were abroad,
he insisted on splitting everything down the middle, even
the double-decker bus fares. That my newly-acquired wealth
would forever put us on unequal footing both infuriated and
frightened him.

I never regretted buying such expensive tennis tickets.
What I did regret was uttering those three insensitive words,
"It's only money." For years, Leo would remind me of them,
telling me how I'd made him feel inadequate. Fortunately,
time has passed. We're two very different people these days,
able to look back on that soggy Sunday and laugh. Now he
remembers those world famous strawberries and clotted
cream with mouth-watering fondness.

### The Short Sale - 2008

Other than that trip to England—when Leo's sobriety
made him edgy about everything—money has never been
the cause of any of our breakups. If Leo wants to add another
pricy guitar to his collection, that's his business. If I want to
shop at secondhand clothing stores, even though I can easily
afford designer labels, that's up to me. We stay out of each
other's buying habits and bank accounts. The issue with us has
to do with me having more money than he does. Leo figures
that automatically gives me power and control over our
relationship.

It never has and it never will.

Still, I worry about this imbalance for Leo's sake. When
he sells his business and moves down here, his income will be
drastically reduced. Even if he gets a good price for his condo
and invests the money wisely, he will still have to watch his

pennies. He's too proud, too stubborn and too independent to want to share my inheritance. Men are funny when it comes to money. Some take it in stride when their mate is wealthier than they are. Others feel castrated by it.

There has to be some way to reduce this inequity.

Sedona is definitely a tourist attraction with its magical vortexes (where people claim they can feel some sort of beneficial energy) and spectacular red rocks. When I first started my snowbird migrations — summering in Vancouver, wintering in the desert — the housing market was booming. In a town where the resident population is roughly ten thousand, there were seven hundred real estate agents. Movie stars like Donald O'Connor and Ann Miller lived here back then. They're both gone now. And so are property values. Still, if you have some ready cash, it's a buyer's paradise.

Maybe real estate is the answer. We could buy a piece of property together and then rent it out. The income would definitely help Leo feel like we're on equal financial footing. When I broach the subject, he seems receptive. There's a real estate office two blocks away so we make an appointment. The agent is waiting for us with a fat folder of possibilities. Her name is Grace and it suits her well.

After we've looked at half a dozen condos in our price range, the seventh one strikes our fancy. A split-level with a shake roof, it has a wood-burning fireplace and a magnificent view. It's only a block away from the main drag in Uptown Sedona so finding renters should be easy. Grace explains that it's a "short sale" which means the bank agrees to take less money than the amount owed on the mortgage. The asking price is a hundred and eighty-four thousand dollars and we, trembling at our own audacity, offer twenty thousand dollars less. Within hours the bank accepts the deal which prompts Leo to transfer twenty-five thousand from his Canadian account into mine.

That gesture means the world to me. For all my outward confidence, a part of me isn't convinced Leo will ever leave Canada. His kids are there. He loves the rain. His business is still thriving. Does he really love me enough to give all that up?

*You never can tell. . . .*

. . .

According to a survey conducted by Citibank, over fifty percent of divorced couples in the United States cited "financial problems" as the primary reason for the demise of their marriage. Leo and I have kept our money separate which is why I believe we've managed to avoid the usual money-wars. Will jointly purchasing this condo jinx that? I doubt it. Still, we love addicts have a powerful need to believe our mates will never take advantage of us.

I knew a woman, another love addict, whose husband was continually in debt. She bailed him out on a regular basis, convinced this would become unnecessary once he learned how to handle his money. He learned, all right. One morning, she discovered her car had been repossessed. The guy had declared bankruptcy, listing her vehicle as one of their joint assets. He also continued racking up bills on her credit card. I checked this out with a lawyer friend and he assured me that, under certain circumstances, it is possible for one spouse to declare bankruptcy without informing the other.

*Will money be an issue?*

I can remember my dad always wanted to take me shopping. I'd refuse to go, explaining that I hated the hassle of trying on clothes that never fit. The real reason had more to do with him using his money to control me. He'd tell me what I should or shouldn't buy, preferring the Lord & Taylor look to my tomboyish choices from the Army Navy Store. Because of this, I understand Leo's discomfort with me being wealthier than he is. I really do. Still, he's had plenty of time to see that I never use my inherited funds to control him. Or make him feel inadequate. His feelings about himself are his feelings and not my responsibility.

# CHAPTER SIX

## What about family and friends?

I don't have children. The members of my immediate family — my sister, dad and mother — are all deceased. Friends, however, are the anchors that have kept my life from drifting off course. Some I've known since childhood. Others have brightened my existence along the way. Most are women but there are also some very supportive brother types. If you asked them about me, they'd probably all agree, "She's eccentric as hell but a damn good friend."

When I've professed my undying love for Leo, they've encouraged me. When I've hated him, they've hated him too. If you shot them full of truth serum right now, I'm sure they would cry in unison, "Not again!" I'm also sure they'd understand why it's imperative for us to try, one last time, to get it right.

Leo doesn't have many friends. He does, however, have a family. A daughter in her forties now and a thirty-something son. When I first met his daughter, she greeted me with, "I don't need another mother." It set the tone for our non-relationship. She acts distant with her dad, too. I suppose his love affair with booze hasn't helped much. His son, on the other hand, treats him like God.

In an article by Dr. Janet G. Woititz about "The 13 Characteristics of Adult Children," she writes, "Adult children of alcoholics are extremely loyal, even in the face of evidence that the loyalty is undeserved." Since Leo (whose dad was an alcoholic) and I (with an alcoholic mother) fit into that category, here are some more characteristics I can certainly relate to:

• Adult children of alcoholics constantly seek approval and affirmation.

• Adult children of alcoholics overreact to changes over which they have no control.
• Adult children have difficulty with intimate relationships.
(And here's one tailor made for Leo.)
• Adult children of alcoholics lie when it would be just as easy to tell the truth.

We have so much history, he and I. Family gatherings…birthday parties…Mother's and Father's Days….. . Frankly, some of these events are best left unremembered.

### Winter Solstice - 1997

I'd only known Leo for three months when he invited me to his family's annual celebration of Winter Solstice. I'd never even heard of Solstice. As far as I was concerned, Christmas wasn't a biggie, either. Joel was Jewish so we didn't bother sending out cards, decorating a tree, or swapping that many presents. This would be my first pagan ritual and I was looking forwad to it. The cast of players included his twenty-three-year-old daughter (whose mother had died when she was seven), his seventeen-year-old son (whose imperious mom was hosting the event) and the daughter's live-in Italian boyfriend. As the days grew shorter and the date got closer, I could feel Leo's tension level rising. He repeatedly made (and misplaced) lists of "Solstice Supplies" :
Cinnamon sticks (to toss in the bonfire)
A dozen oranges
Whole cloves (to stick in the oranges)
Red, green, yellow candles (to create a Medieval effect)
Holly branches (to weave into napkin holders, I think)
The plan was for him to stay over at his ex's place the night before. As he loaded up the van, he smacked his forehead as if to spank his own bad memory. He forgot the cloves. More tension in the air. Plus a major snowstorm was predicted for later that evening.
Promising to follow his over-explained directions, I assure him I'll be there around eleven o'clock the next morning. Driving conditions didn't worry me. I grew up

with black ice and snowdrifts that blanketed our dining room windows. The thought of him staying overnight at his ex's didn't threaten me a bit. She'd gotten morbidly obese and, besides, they hated each other too much to wind up in the same bed. As Leo slammed the van door shut after making sure the holly boughs were safely secured, I told him that, if they needed something else, I could always bring it tomorrow.

"That won't be necessary," he snapped.

Was I imagining things or did he resent me being part of his family's Solstice?

It snowed all night. Motorists were advised to stay off the Trans-Canada Highway since freezing temperatures had made the roads even more treacherous. His daughter, who hated these family gatherings, phoned and said she couldn't make it. His son, who lived for them, said he'd be there even if he had to come by dog sled.

When I finally arrived, shaken by so many close calls and unavoidable skids, Leo was nowhere to be found. He was out "blessing the trees," according to his ex. She was stringing strands of cranberries together, her pumpkin face already aglow from too much mulled cider. We chatted about nothing for what seemed like forever, when Leo wafted through the doorway.

Oh dear. It was going to be a long day, indeed.

Their son kept phoning every fifteen minutes, apologizing for his absence, outlining in detail which route he was planning to attempt next. I tried to keep the celebratory mood going by asking questions about Solstice—who the Druids were, what holly branches symbolized—but the room reeked of disappointment.

Before I left, the three of us did a closing ceremony where we each shared our hopes and good wishes for the New Year. It was a painful experience and one I would be expected to repeat year after year. I made it through three more Solstices and then I quit going. My absence was hardly noticed. When I had gone to these sacred family gatherings, nobody asked me a single question. Where I was living? What I was working on? How Leo and I were getting along? His family is definitely weird. Then again, whose family isn't.

### West Hartford, Connecticut – Spring of '97

When the invitation to my nephew's wedding arrived, I jumped at the chance to introduce my new man to the family. By this time, my alcoholic mother had died. My living family members consisted of a father (well into his nineties), an older sister (who hadn't always approved of the men I'd brought home) and her two children, a daughter and a son. The other two players were my sister's first husband (who raised their kids after she left him) and her current husband (the man she ran off with).

"Your nephew sure looks like your sister's current husband," Leo told me, after he'd met the groom-to-be. The resemblance was remarkable. Years before, I asked my sister about this and she confessed that she'd been intimate with both men at the time of her son's conception. DNA didn't exist back then and even if it had, her first husband deserves full marks for being the boy's real dad regardless of bloodlines.

I was slightly nervous presenting this blue collar boyfriend, who hadn't even finished college, to my Yalie dad and my sister — a *magna cum laude* graduate of Vassar. I needn't have been. When Leo wants to, he can charm the skin off a rattler with his "Aww shucks" Southern drawl.

Of course there were other issues going on behind the scenes. My father was at an age where only he thought he was a good driver. The rest of the family refused to ride with him. When I insisted Leo chauffeur us to the wedding, Dad pouted loudly from the back seat. He got over his senior tantrum eventually but not soon enough for my taste.

The wedding was opulent in a muted, well-orchestrated sort of way. We were assigned seats under a huge tent and given throw away Kodak cameras to preserve the occasion. Leo and I drank ourselves into a satisfying stupor, pretending to be fascinated by cousin John's stories about his four sons' greatest accomplishments. We threw the required confetti at my nephew and his barbie doll bride, as they fled the scene on their way to Maui.

There is no bad ending to this story. Everyone was relieved that I'd finally found a mate who was earning a decent living, loved me, and made me laugh. Even my best girlfriend from earliest childhood approved of him. Flying back to Canada, I felt complete — having at long last found my Prince Charming. Four months later, we'd be flying back to Canada again, my broken arm wrapped in a makeshift sling.

### Shades of *The Exorcist* - 1997

This incident happened between my nephew's wedding and our fateful trip to New York City. We butted heads a lot but co-writing the screenplay gave us something creative to share. Still, Leo needed his "alone time" and I needed a break from trying to be perfect. I'd make dinner dates with various girlfriends. Meeting my male friends wasn't worth the snide remarks I'd get from Leo later about what I was really doing.

Two weeks earlier, I'd bumped into an old roommate in a local supermarket. She had two small kids in tow and we promised to get together soon. Soon was tonight. Over several carafes of red wine, Tina (not her real name) caught me up on the chaos in her life. She was currently getting divorced from a cocaine-addicted husband, hoping his wealthy but enabling parents would contribute child support. I, on the other hand, just raved on and on about Leo and our charmed lives. After three hours, we were too drunk to drive.

I phoned Leo and asked him to come get us.

"I can't wait for you to meet Tina!" I slurred, extolling her brilliant impression of Linda Blair in the movie *The Exorcist*.

"I can't wait either," he slurred back.

We only lived a few blocks away and, as it turned out, Tina lived a mile further down the road on the same street. When Leo pulled up, I flung myself like a sack of flour into the back seat. I wanted Tina to sit beside him so he could get the full impact of her Linda Blair impression. She put on her best devil-voice and began spewing forth swear words. I roared with laughter, delighted that this dear friend had resurfaced. When Leo pulled up to the curb, she jumped out quickly, promising to call the next day.

I didn't hear from her for months.

It wasn't until after Leo and I had broken up that Tina

revealed what had happened on that short ride home. She's a busty blonde full of fun and enthusiasm. If she dropped fifty pounds, she could be a model or a movie star. As she sat in the passenger seat doing her best Linda Blair impression, Leo grabbed her left breast with his right hand and began fondling it, tweaking her nipple with his finger.

All through dinner, I'd raved about this man, how he was the "real deal," my "knight in shining armor." She didn't have the heart to burst my bubble. She also knew enough about men to know that he would never, in a million years, tell me what had transpired that night. She was right. He never did. Years later, when I questioned him about it, he defended himself with a wink, saying, "She asked for it."

My first thought was, "What an asshole!"

But then, as I began thinking about it, he probably interpreted Tina's Linda Blair imitation, all that foul language, as a kind of raunchy come-on. Leo was also very drunk and so were we. It's not like that now. He and I are both sober — and very much accountable for our actions.

We want this relationship to succeed more than anything.

I believe our families and friends do, too.

An ex roommate keeps saying I'm not myself when Leo's around. I talk faster, laugh nervously. Maybe so but I think many of us, especially women, behave differently when our man intermingles with family and friends. We want their approval a little too much.

...

I read another relationship survey online conducted by *DivorceMagazine.com* claiming that, six percent of the respondents felt their in-laws were "fully responsible" for their divorce. Thirty-five percent said their former spouse's parents were either "mostly or somewhat responsible" for the breakup of their marriage. If I had intrusive in-laws, I'd probably feel the same way.

Stepchildren are another stumbling block. I've been lucky there, too. Other than Leo's unfriendly daughter, the offspring of my former lovers have been welcoming and warm. I've also never been involved with someone whose kids are living with him. That can cause all sorts of problems.

Take my friend Matt and his stepsons. "If I told those boys to quit doing something, they'd say, 'You're not my dad. You can't tell me what to do!'" Matt's wife would simply shrug her shoulders and say, "They're Jeff's kids.'"

At one point, her eight-year-old began showing signs of physical as well as mental difficulties. Not wanting to make waves, Matt kept his mouth shut until the boy started stabbing him in the arm with a pocket knife and shooting at him with a pellet gun. That's when he left the marriage. But two years later, goaded on by loneliness, Matt stepped back into the relationship." I built this brand new home for us, just us, and her kids wouldn't move out." He pauses, unable to let go of the hurt." Two of her boys are still living with her at age thirty and thirty-six."

*What about family and friends?*

I can't imagine following my friends' advice over the advice of my own heart. In the past, when Leo and I have broken up, they've expressed relief. (When they were sure the break was official! ) Now, I notice a shift in attitude. Maybe it's because we aren't rushing into anything. I'm not pushing him to come down here before he's ready. And he's not getting defensive about it, either. We're following AA's suggestion and taking it *"One day at a time."* If this re-relationship was brand new, I'd understand my friends' and family's skepticism. But a lasting togetherness can turn even the worst memories into beautiful ones.

# CHAPTER SEVEN

## Why is our relationship different this time?

By now, I'm sure you have your own opinion about whether Leo and I will make it or not. The romantics are probably hopeful. The realists, doubtful. I'm on the side of the Hopeful Romantics. I believe people do change, that a destructive relationship can ultimately reverse itself.

### Vancouver – Early Mornings

Leo and I always clink coffee cups at the beginning of these morning phone chats. It's our way of being together from a thousand, five hundred and eleven miles apart. I usually call him but if I'm more than a few minutes late, he calls me.

"You're late. Did I wake you up? "

"As a matter of fact, you did. But it's okay."

"How're you doing? " Leo waits eagerly for my response. If I'm happy, he's happy. If I'm not, he wants to help me get there.

"I had this incredible dream but it's gone now. Something about hiking and ice cream."

"Were you on a Rocky Road? "

I wince at his pun, quick to counter with, "No. But I did listen to some Cherry Garcia on the radio last night."

He groans and we're off on a punning jag. "I prefer Milly Vanilla myself."

"Sure, Burt."

Leo pauses. I can hear the wheels clicking. "There was this little girl, see. And she had this tin can that she peed in. Well then a goat came along and he butt her pee can. Butter pecan, get it? "

"I got it, I got it. And it's giving me a chocolate chip on

my shoulder."

Leo's running late for work today, so we opt for only one meditation reading instead of the usual two. Sharing these passages makes me feel closer to him. This one's about reality. The author speaks of "making contact with something or someone outside of ourselves to ground us."

"You're my reality check," Leo says, before discussing the pros and cons of moving to Sedona. When he's finished, I reflect on my realities. Right now, I'm feeling grateful. For life. For my health. But mostly for our commitment to one another. In the past, I used to try and keep Leo on the phone beyond his capacity to listen. Now I intuitively sense when it's time to trade "I-love-you's" and hang up.

### Sedona -Saturday Afternoons

Time for our weekly lovemaking. Although Leo would prefer a less structured sex schedule, he's learned to accept and appreciate it. We're older now. He worries about how long it will take him to have an orgasm. I worry about wanting him inside me—and yet knowing the pain isn't worth it. No matter how many years we've been coupling, there's always a little uncertainty beforehand.

"Backrub time!" I tell him, pulling off his undershirt and ordering him to lie on his stomach. I pretend to be a professional masseuse. His back is slightly misshapen due to a childhood case of spinal meningitis. He never used to let me give him massages, claiming he was ashamed of it. Now he actually enjoys them.

One of his toes got broken playing football and never healed properly. When I begin massaging his feet, his body stiffens. "Don't worry, I'll be careful," I whisper. His feet are splendiferous. Long, slender and perfectly sculpted.

When he turns over on his back, I continue playing the part of a disinterested masseuse. He never knows when my touch will turn sexual. Neither do I. Then it happens—I want him hard. For me, his excitement is reward enough. For Leo, he wants me aroused as well. My orgasms are quick and tidy. A few soundless moans and it's finished. Now it's his turn. Leo literally roars like a lion when he climaxes.

In the aftermath of our intimacy, he whispers, "Thank you."

I feel connected to him in a way words can't express. Our love-making sessions are less gymnastic these days, but the closeness that follows hasn't changed. While he's drifting in and out of consciousness, I slip away thinking to myself, "How many couples, who've been together as long as we have, still feel this incredible bond after sex? "

### Dining Out – Anytime,Anywhere

Many couples when they dine out are silent. The only sounds you hear are food-related. The crunch-crunch of lettuce being chewed, the scraping of knives against plates. This isn't the case with us. There's a lot of laughter and lively conversation. I always order the same thing. Leo usually orders something different. When our meal arrive he'll reach across the table with exaggerated curiosity, hoping for a bite of my taco salad.

"Watch that!" I'll cry, fending him off with my fork.

"Just a taste? "

"No way, José."

He doesn't really want one. He just loves teasing me. Like a kid in school who stuffs a rubber spider in some girl's backpack.

"See that guy over there? " He motions toward a couple sitting at another booth. The man is wearing a loud, Hawaiian shirt.

"What about him? "

"He's just won the lottery."

"Really!"

"The lady he's with is not his wife," Leo continues, polishing off another shrimp. "He's afraid that if he tells her he's won, she'll threaten to tell his wife unless he gives her half the money."

"Smart cookie," I say, looking around the restaurant for someone else to make up a story about. Another diner waves the waitress over. He could easily pass for Dean Martin's younger brother. "See that man over there? "

"Yeah? "

"He's a wise guy."

"Really!"

"He's been watching those other two like a hawk, and he senses something isn't quite *kosher*."

"If he's Italian, what does he know from *kosher*? "

We chuckle and fall temporarily silent, enjoying the rest of our meals. Even though I'm petite, my ability to pack in food is impressive. Wolfing down what's left of my shredded chicken, I snap the taco shell in half and devour that, too. Leo's eating style is more moderate. He rarely finishes everything so he'll ask the waitress for a doggie bag. In the old days, I used to get upset by this. I'm not exactly sure why. Now I welcome it, as his leftovers will save me a trip to the supermarket tomorrow.

"Will there be anything else this evening, sir? "

"No thanks. Just the check, please."

When the waitress hands Leo the bill, he looks at the total in mock horror, clutching at his chest. He's been pulling this same routine ever since I've known him. Doesn't matter whether we're in a five-star restaurant or Denny's. How I love these childish games of his — and he loves me for loving them.

As we walk home, the desert sky sparkles with clarity. Leo points out the Big Dipper and when I gaze upward, he kisses me. I'm momentarily caught off guard but then I return his tenderness with some of my own. We've witnessed so many full moons and so many shooting stars through the years.

...

It's hard to give up the good times even when the bad ones start outweighing them. I used to cling to those good times like a frightened kid holding onto her mama's hand the first day of school. I'd tell myself that whatever had gone wrong was my fault and I had the ability to fix it. There's a saying that goes, "*To let go is to fear less and love more.*" That's been a real challenge for both of us. We definitely do have fun together. And when our love is right, it couldn't be righter. But letting go of control, simply accepting life on life's terms, is never easy.

*Why is our relationship different this time?*

Leo no longer lies. I no longer try to control him. I also think age is factor. We're both very aware of our own mortality. Of time running out. How many more chances will we get? There's a definite comfort level between us, too. We know each other's histories, the highlights and low lights of our lives. Which childhood trauma still hurts. Which accomplishment has meant the most. Our medical concerns, family secrets, his unfulfilled dreams and aspirations. When I look at Leo, I see the young man I first fell in love with. To others, he may seem old and vulnerable. To me, he will always be virile, handsome and the hero of my fairytale.

# PART TWO – REALITY

As I was sitting in my chair
I knew the bottom wasn't there
Nor legs nor back, but I just sat,
Ignoring little things like that.

- Hughes Mearns -

# CHAPTER EIGHT

## Am I being realistic?

What motivates people's perceptions? Why do love addicts see a bad guy as someone to be saved? Or an emotionally unavailable partner as someone who, with enough love and understanding, will come around? I've had my quota of unworkable relationships and the last thing I need right now is another one. It's time to examine more closely who I've chosen in the past and why. Am I simply repeating the pattern learned as a child, of picking men who will unlove me to death?

*You never can tell.*

### Songwriting in the 60's

We've all had a crush on someone who's either married or involved with somebody else. We may not act on those feelings but I'm convinced every woman has them at some point. My Mister Unavailable was a music publisher. After graduating from college, I moved to Manhattan to become a professional songwriter. I worked in advertizing for awhile. Then a guitar shop, where I ran a music school. The streets were teeming with talented people, hoping to sell yet another potential chartbuster.

The first time I met Stanley was on the tenth floor of the Brill Building at 1619 Broadway. The Brill Building housed many successful songwriters as well as publishers. When I was trying to make it in the music biz, the most famous of them was Donny Kirschner, whose writing stable included Carole King, Neil Diamond and Neil Sedaka. As I marched into Stanley's office, I couldn't help but notice all the framed gold records, pop standards like "I Will Wait For You" and "Goin' Out Of My Head." I also noticed him checking me out.

Sitting at the upright piano, I played him three of my best songs. He offered me a fifty dollar advance against royalties for one called "Lie A Little" that was eventually recorded by jazz singer Morgana King. It also became the theme song for our three year love affair.

Stanley was thirteen years older than I was and not my usual tall, lanky, Clint Eastwood type. Chunky, with meaty hands and a wise-cracking manner, he and his brother had had a tap-dancing act when he was younger. They'd even appeared on screen in one of those Bob Hope *On The Road* pics. How I loved listening to his showbiz stories. We'd meet for drinks after work. Him, with his vodka martini extra dry; me, with a Dubonnet on the rocks. Not wanting to fall into the category of a married man's afternoon delight, I refused to be intimate with him for nearly a year. My goal was simple. I wanted him to divorce his wife and marry me.

Like most unfaithful husbands, Stanley's complaints were pretty standard. No sexual chemistry between him and his wife. He assured me they'd stopped having sex. I believed him until she got pregnant. Then he promised that the upcoming birth of his son would not stop him from leaving the marriage. I believed that one too.

After we'd been together two and a half years, I gave him an ultimatum: "If you really love me, you'll arrange to meet with my dad and tell him you want to marry me." It was my way of testing how honorable his intentions were. Stanley and my dad met for a drink at The Oak Room in the now Trumpified Plaza Hotel.

Filled with impatience and a sense of impending doom, I waited for my father's report.

"The man's in a tough spot," he told me over the phone. "It's his second marriage, his wife is pregnant. They've been trying to have a baby for eight years." Pausing to clear his throat, he added, "And she's still working while he tries to establish — "

"I know all that!" I interrupted. None of it mattered to me. What my dad said next mattered terribly.

"I don't see him giving all that up for you."

He was right, of course. But like the first song I'd sold Stanley, I wanted my dad to lie a little.

For me, there's something addicting about trying to get what you can't have. Like a kid begging to stay up past his bedtime. Whether this desire is based on an overblown ego, or an under developed one, it's been an ongoing pattern of mine for as long as I can remember.

### After My First Divorce – In the 80's

For a love addict, whose romantic needs are often unrealistic and short-lived, the relationship I had with my first husband Joel lasted a long time. Fourteen years. He was a songwriter and so was I. We met in New York through a mutual friend and, six months later, got married in Los Angeles at city hall. He had a writing partner who consumed all of Joel's waking hours, which made any kind of bond between us superficial at best. Still, it gave me time to pursue my writing career rather than play Little Miss Wifey. I remember how shocked our families were when I didn't change my last name. In hindsight, that action alone describes how separate our lives were.

But this isn't about Joel.

It's about Dee, a man I still consider to be the love of my life.

When I noticed that his mom had locks on her bedroom door I should have been suspicious. By then, however, I was too emotionally invested. Dee could have hidden a loaded gun under his pillow and I would've convinced myself somebody else had left it there.

I was separated from Joel by now. After years and years of trying to wrestle him away from his writing partner, I'd had it. We bought a cabin up in Lake Arrowhead, California but never managed to use it for more than a few days at a time. When we did, the next door neighbor was always coming over wanting to use the phone. He was an eccentric fellow with an arsenal of wild tales. I nicknamed him Diesel because he was always running on fumes.

Diesel had some pretty unusual tattoos, terrible teeth and eyes that could burn a hole right through you. He scared a lot of people off with his tough guy demeanor and dire predictions about the future. But I never took any of that seriously. To me, he was just a colorful character. And when he let down his guard, he was very entertaining.

Once I became officially separated from my husband, our friendship blossomed into something more. Dee's world — one of poverty, drugs and crime — was a far cry from the one Joel and I had created for ourselves, watching *The Love Boat* and *Fantasy Island* every Saturday night. When we started living together, I noticed his mood swings immediately. In the mornings, he'd have to go out on the porch and smoke a couple of Pall Malls before he could manage a curt "Howdy." By evening, he'd be his affable self. I just assumed he wasn't a morning person. But the longer we lived together, the more I realized his moods were too extreme to be caused by waking up foggy-minded. When I asked him about it, he was evasive.

Dee was evasive about a lot of things.

When Joel and I first got to know him, he'd mentioned something vague about being in jail a couple of times. We thought it was kind of exciting. Like a character in a movie played by Lee Marvin or Jack Palance. Later on, when he knew I was hooked on loving him, he confessed that he'd spent over half his life in juvie and federal prisons. He'd even landed a non-speaking part in Woody Allen's "*Take the Money and Run,*" filmed on location at San Quentin. Nothing he could tell me about his past would've mattered by then. I'd already given him a hundred and ten percent of my heart.

That's also when he decided to come clean about his thirty year heroin habit.

I'd never known a dope fiend before. Not unless you count Frank Sinatra's portrayal of Frankie in *The Man With the Golden Arm.* Movies have always been my frame of reference. Dee's had more to do with robbing his own mother to pay for more junk.

After wrapping my head around this unwanted piece of truth, I went back to college to earn my alcohol and drug counseling certificate. Degree in hand, I got a job at the local hospital as an intake counselor. This gave me a legitimate excuse to urge my partner to sign up as an out-patient. The first week he met with his counselor — an ex heroin addict himself — the guy begged Dee to bring him some weed from down the hill next time they met.

So much for recovery.

I went to court to help him see his kids on weekends. Their fundamentalist mother (a woman who routinely asked Jesus for driving directions rather than consult a map) would only allow their father visitation privileges if I was present. In effect, I became their second mom. Johnny and Anita were only three and five at the time and I suddenly developed a real reverence for MacDonalds.

Aside from my mother's alcoholism, this was my first foray into loving an addict. It was also my first boomerang relationship. We'd break up when he was using and reunite when he was clean. I honestly believed my love would be enough for him to quit.

It never was.

Ultimately, he moved to Rogue River, Oregon where his family owned a bit of land. I was living in LA at the time, dating a tennis player. Just as we were about to take off for a Davis Cup tournament in Hartford, Connecticut, some inner voice told me I should cancel my flight and drive directly to Oregon. I followed my gut. Thirteen hours later, as I pulled wearily into his weed-littered driveway, Dee's expression at seeing me was all the reward I needed.

He'd been clean eight months. He'd even quit smoking. Still, his skin had a grayish tint that had me concerned. The next morning, he collapsed. We rushed to the Emergency Room in Medford where they began giving him a myriad of tests. Because he had a history of heroin use and AIDS was a relatively new disease, his room was quarantined. By the time the results came back, I'd returned to LA to take his two kids to the circus. He phoned me with the verdict: terminal cancer. Six months later, Diesel was dead. If he were alive today, I'd probably still be with him. And if he was using, I'd probably still be trying to straighten him out.

### Summer of 2007

I met Paul online shortly after I'd gone to Leo's apartment and tried to save him from himself. Fearing that his pleading emails might weaken my resolve, I immediately attached myself to this good-looking silver fox who lived in

Anaheim, California. Like the guy from Switzerland, he was another engineer who'd fallen on hard times and now worked as a live-in caregiver. He was a superb classical pianist and every night, via telephone, he'd play me something by Chopin or Debussy to lull me to sleep.

Often with these online liaisons everything gets blown out of proportion. Men and women declare their undying love before they've even met. When they do meet, there's zero chemistry. Paul and I weren't able to see each other face-to-face for several months because I was still summering in Canada. Instead, we wrote these long, self-revealing emails and conversed by phone for hours. I developed a pack of reservations about Paul but managed to keep them at bay. One, he was sixty-three and had never been married. Two, he wasn't close to any of his family and had very few friends. The worst thing about him, however, was his voice. It sounded like a whiny child, always wanting, "More ice cream, Mommy. More ice cream!"

Still, he was crazy about me. We were already using the "L" word, planning the rest of our lives together. He told me one thing, however, that made me a bit queasy. "I want to be like a cocker spaniel sitting at your feet. I won't bother you, I just need to be close by." Something about that statement didn't sound right.

Oh well. Maybe he had a special thing for dogs.

We arranged to meet in person when I returned to Arizona for the winter. He flew to Phoenix and I drove down to pick him up. Grabbing a bite to eat on the way back to Sedona, we cuddled up in the booth like budgies in a birdcage. The waitress remarked how she wished she could be as in love as we looked when she was our age. I didn't like the age reference, but the other part fit right in with my concept of togetherness. Paul stayed with me for two weeks. I got used to his whiny voice and his cocker spaniel ways but I knew, in my heart of hearts, it would never work.

Nonetheless, I conned myself into trying. He was musical, and so was I. He liked to over analyze things and I did, too. He'd had prostate cancer and wasn't that sexually active. A match made in heaven, right?

Whenever we'd argue, Paul would burst into tears.

I found this very disconcerting. Still, we decided he should move in with me for a three month trial period. His stuff became another red flag. Paul was a packrat whereas I'm a minimalist. Clutter is anathema to me. When he confessed that he hated to give up a life-sized statue of Tinkerbell he'd found at a garage sale, I should've walk away. When he sent his ex girlfriend of eight years a Christmas card and she sent it back unopened, I should have walked away. When he told me he'd had sex with the eighty-five-year-old woman he was supposedly looking after, I should have run like hell. Instead, I told myself, " Compared to her body, mine's got to look great!" After the relationship ended, I vowed never to let myself get into another unrealistic situation like that again.

...

　　　I've had my share of therapy. When I was seeing Stanley, I began working with a psychologist in New York's Upper East Side. She encouraged me to examine my pattern of equating love with unavailability. After all, my father was a workaholic and my mom, a boozer. What kind of emotional support could either of them offer me? It made a lot of sense. Still, I wasn't ready to change my behavior. I wanted the lady to tell me how I could get Stanley to leave his wife. When she couldn't, I quit going.

　　　My next therapeutic experience revolved around Dee's drug use. He and I both went to see an addictions counselor in Redlands, California. When he started using heroin again, I continued seeing Dr. Siddons on my own. He tried to point out how addicted I was becoming to the negative excitement Dee provided.

　　　"That's ridiculous," I told him. "I simply want to help him stay clean!"

　　　At one point, my therapist said, "Either you stop seeing Dee, or you stop seeing me." The choice was easy. I quit going.

　　　When you live in Canada, seeing a psychiatrist is free. (That is, if your regular doctor prescribes it.) Leo and I had been through at least two breakups when I suggested we seek professional help. The psychiatrist had a foreign accent that made his English nearly impossible to understand. But he loved the cinema. By the third session, he was urging us to quit drinking. I would have none of it. They say alcoholism is the disease of denial. Well, I was not about to face the fact that drinking was ruining our relationship. It took another three years and an overnight blackout before I could admit I had a serious drinking problem. Then I quit and everything changed.

*Am I being realistic?*

I think so. Or, I could be doing what my Welsh granny used to refer to as, *"Turning a sow's ear into a silk purse."* The way I see it, Leo and I have spent a major portion of our lives together. We've experienced getting sober; the deaths of both our dads; the disappointment of breaking up, the elation of reconnecting. After fifteen years of trying, we should know what works — and what doesn't. One thing I do know, I'd rather rescue a thirsty plant by giving it water than try to save a dying relationship.

# CHAPTER NINE

## Who was I growing up?

### FAMILY TIES

Those ties were broken in my troubled youth
As I stood tough, jaw clenched and posture proud.
I claimed my independence long and loud
From anything that smacked of being couth.
Or had the ring of some parental truth.
I wore my hatred like a body shroud.
A trouble-maker hoping for a crowd,
The biblical antithesis of Ruth.
And still I seek approval from his grave,
Those gentle words my father left unsaid.
If only I might find a wand to wave
To rouse this rigid man from playing dead.
"You know I didn't mean to misbehave."
The breezes sigh. A lily shakes its head.

- Jill Williams -

"You and your sister will never have a successful
relationship with a man. You're both too selfish." That's what
our father used to tell us, but my sister proved him wrong.
Her second marriage was a perfect union. And until her
untimely death, she and her husband were devoted to each
other. I think a lot of my relationships have been successful
as well. My first marriage lasted nearly fifteen years and, for
the majority of that time, Joel and were quite happy. Still, my
dad's dictum stung. Who knows why he said what he did?
We probably hadn't made our beds or done our homework.
But I agree with him. I am too selfish to have the kind of
relationship he would have considered successful. I'm just not

cut out to be a Stepford Wife who presses her hubby's shirts
and makes certain his steak is served medium rare.
      My parents did the best they were capable of doing.
I don't blame them for why I developed a knack for picking
(and sticking with) wrong relationships. This is not about
being a victim of the past. It's important for me — as a love
addict — to pinpoint certain incidents that define who I was
growing up.

### The Night Before Christmas – Early Childhood

      We're perched on the staircase, my sister and I,
listening to our parents argue. I keep trying to squeeze my
four-year-old head through the bannister bars but it won't fit.
My sister looks scared.
      "What's wrong? " I ask her.
      "Nothing."
      I can tell she's worried. She has a wide forehead and
when she's unhappy it wrinkles. My mother's doing most of
the talking but the library door is shut, so we can't understand
what she's saying.
      "I wish they wouldn't fight." Sis picks at the skin
around her fingernails. Even though she's four years older, I
feel more grown up most of the time.
      "I wish they wouldn't too," I say, picking at my own
nails.
      She pauses, sucking her finger where it's starting to
bleed." I wonder what they're fighting about."
      "Mommy's drinking."
      "What? "
      "That's what they're always fighting about," I tell her.
      Suddenly I feel sleepy." I'm going to bed. Merry
Christmas."
      "Merry Christmas," she whispers softly, more to
herself than to me.
      My sister looks so sad sitting on the stairs.
      I wish I could make her feel better.

### Skeet Shooting With My Dad

"Pull!" I powder it. I love spending Sunday afternoons with my dad at the gun club. I'm the son he never had — despite his insistence that he's perfectly happy with two beautiful daughters.

"Pull!" I powder another one. The man standing next to my dad says something complimentary about me. Daddy beams with pride. I may be a girl but thanks to his coaching I'm a damn fine shot. And he's a good teacher. He knows when to push, and when to give you a pat on the shoulder. I love the feel of the twelve-gauge he lets me borrow. It's a Browning over and under with intricate etchings where the barrel breaks open. My sister has the smarts in our family. I'm the jock. Out here, wrapped in winter clothing and drinking hot chocolate in between rounds, my dad seems much more relaxed. I can understand why. For these few hours he doesn't have to deal with my mother's snide comments.

"Oh my god! That's Fred Blackall," I whisper, hiding behind my dad. I've had a crush on that boy for two summers.

"Why don't you go over and say hello to him? " my dad asks.

"I couldn't."

"Why not? "

"He might think I like him."

"I thought you did."

"I do!" My dad shakes his head, confused as usual by female logic. I watch in horror, as Fred approaches. At seventeen, he still has the gawkiness of youth but his smile is ageless. And those dark, wavy curls are delicious. I may only be thirteen but he makes me feel a lot older.

"Hey there, Fred. How're you doing? "

Very well, Mr. Williams." He turns to me and smiles"

"You wanna shoot some targets? "

"I—I—sure!" I look at my dad. "What do I use for a rifle?"

"I have one you can borrow," Fred replies." Meet me out at the range in five minutes. Okay? "

"Okay."

As soon as Fred leaves the clubhouse, my dad turns to

me and gives me the strangest piece of advice. "If you want that boy to ask you out, don't beat him."

"What?" I wasn't sure I heard right.

"Men of any age don't like women who make them look bad."

"But you've always told me to be the best I can be. What do you mean 'don't beat him'?"

"Just what I said." With that, my father walked away.

Target practice is a lot different than skeet or trap shooting. Still, I had a steady hand and a good aim. Pretty soon my shots were getting closer and closer to the bullseye. I was concentrating so hard I forgot all about being shy.

I also forgot to follow my dad's advice.

By the end, my scores were better than Fred's. I knew then that he would never ask me out on a date. And he never did.

As an adult, my competitive nature has caused me untold grief in the love department. Whether I'm playing gin rummy or tennis, I can't stand to lose. Worse, I can't stand to let somebody else win on purpose. It's lying.

### On the Drive Home from "The Lighthouse"

We were at the shore. My dad would rent a seaside cottage in Groton, Connecticut for June, July and August. He'd come down on weekends and the rest of the time we were left to enjoy the benefits of The Shennecossett Beach Club. That summer, my sixteen-year-old sister had her first serious boyfriend. His name was George Hastings and this weekend he was coming down from West Hartford to visit her. George was very tall and *very* handsome. I kept telling myself, "When I'm older, I want a boyfriend just like him!"

This incident took place on a Friday night. George, my sister, my mother and I were going to New London to have dinner at a restaurant in a lighthouse. I remember it had this humongous lobster hanging on the wall above the entrance. (They claimed it weighed in at forty-three pounds.)

After we'd eaten, my mother was too drunk to drive so George got behind the wheel of her turquoise Studebaker. I sat in back with Mommy, my sister was in the passenger seat beside George.

Whenever our mother drinks, she has two moods: amorous or bitchy. Tonight she's feeling amorous. She's a small woman, under five feet, whose waistline has gotten considerably wider since childbirth. She maintains having babies is the reason she gained weight. It's our fault she's so fat.

All of a sudden she leans forward, wraps her arms around George's neck, and starts whispering in his ear. The poor guy is driving so he can't do anything but watch the road. My sister is mortified.

I'm just plain pissed. "Cut it out!" I hiss at her.

She ignores me, continuing to run her chubby fingers through George's wavy brown hair. I want to leap over and pull her off of him, but I know that'll only make the situation worse.

"Please, Mommy," I plead, "leave the poor guy alone."

By now, my sister is whimpering in the front seat, convinced George won't ever want to see her again. My mother thinks the whole thing is funny, insisting that all she was doing was telling him what a good driver he was. Looking directly at me and smiling, she says. "We had a lovely dinner so I suggest you cool down and stop making a mountain out of a molehill."

I wanted to argue back but I felt so sorry for my sister I kept my mouth shut.

We drove the rest of the way home in silence.

I knew my mother had a drinking problem but I didn't know what an alcoholic was. Or why she could never seem to stop after one drink. Later, I learned a lot of things. About alcoholism, my father's mistress, how my parent's firstborn died five days after she came into this world. Because my mother was extremely ill after giving birth, the doctors advised my dad not to tell her. Not until her own health improved. I don't think Mommy ever forgave him for that. Like I said before, they did the best they could.

*Who was I growing up?*

I was a fighter and a survivor. I still am. I could share

many examples of my rebellious nature: cajoling everyone in my senior class to dye their hair green on St. Patrick's Day; driving my dad's Eldorado Cadillac backwards to my best friend's house before I had a driver's license; inviting a black guy to escort me to my debutante party. As the second (surviving) child in our dysfunctional family, I was what is commonly referred to as "The Scapegoat" or "The Acting Out Child."

According to an article written by Robert Burney (" Roles In Dysfunctional Families" ), the scapegoat is the most emotionally honest child in the family, acts out the tension and anger the family ignores, provides distraction from the real issues in the family and often has trouble in school because they get attention the only way they know how – which is negatively. Burney's last observation reads, "They often become pregnant or addicted as teenagers." Luckily, that wasn't the case with me. My addictions came later. So did Leo's. He is also the scapegoat in his dysfunctional family.

# CHAPTER TEN

## Which parent am I trying to replicate?

There's a theory that women pick partners who mirror their fathers. My dad was an extrovert. Persistent when it came to selling life insurance. Enthusiastic. A rebel in his own way since his closest friend was Jewish, despite strong anti-Semitism in our community. But the men I've picked as partners have more of my mother's traits. A keen wit. Very creative. She was also vulnerable and maddeningly manipulative.

In Leo's case he definitely picked me because I reminded him of his mother. She was musical. Impulsive. Funny. (And terrified of her sexually inappropriate father.) I remember when I first met Leo's family and they showed me old photos of her, the physical resemblance was startling. I looked just like his mother. We even struck the same comic poses when being photographed. His story is the classic Oedipal one where he was his Mama's hero until his dad returned from World War II. Leo was three or four at the time and never quite got over it. She was also sexually inappropriate with him which has left some serious scars on his psyche. Not so different, really, from the ones my mother left on my psyche. She had her good points, though.

### Fairy Gardens

"I put mine out already! Did you? "My sister nodded in the affirmative.

Every Friday night our mother would give us each a pan in which to build a fairy garden. She claimed that if we made them inviting enough — with plenty of soft moss, pebbled pathways, maybe an acorn or two to sit on — the fairies would come and dance away the night. The creation of these mini ballrooms was indescribably fun. "I pushed thumbtacks in the moss for the fairies to sit on."

"I used toothpicks," my sister countered. "So they can string lanterns."

I'm not sure I believed in those fairies but I wanted to. The really exciting part came the following morning. We'd scramble downstairs to see if the fairies had partied in our gardens. Sometimes they would. Other times, no. When they did, the thumbtacks would be upturned, the toothpicks broken in half. It was my mother who'd sneak outside after we were in bed and make the fairy-messes that delighted us so.

### My First and Last Séance

I was sixteen. I'd invited two really cute Lacrosse players from Deerfield Academy over to my house to try and bring back Albert Einstein from the dead. My girlfriend and I wanted to do something different, not just spin records and dance.

We had a playroom in the basement where I set up a card table and four chairs. I'd read some booklet about how to conduct a séance so I became the resident expert. All I lacked was a crystal ball and a turban. The four of us locked hands and touched knees so nobody could cheat.

"Albert Einstein, if you can hear us, knock three times!" I tried to sound serious but it was all I could do not to burst out laughing. Everybody else was properly earnest.

"Albert Einstein," I intoned again. "If you can hear us, knock three times."

The room was eerily quiet. Nobody believed he would knock.

For a third time, I spoke in hallowed tones. "Albert Einstein! If you can hear us, knock three times!"

Tap, tap, tap. We froze in fear. The boys' studied indifference changed to panic, My girlfriend screamed. I jumped up and said, "Let's get outta here!"

It wasn't until years later that my mother confessed she'd gone outside and tapped three times with a broom handle on our basement window. I was slightly peeved with her for scaring us like that. But looking back now, I think it was quite clever of her. I can tell you one thing, I never went to another séance.

## Mommy's Morning Orange Juice

It always smelled funny. Nothing like the fresh-squeezed orange juice my father insisted on every morning. Had I known what vodka tasted like, and how it didn't make your breath reek of alcohol,' I might have figured it out.

She had her own bedroom and my father had his. In the twenty-three years they were married, I never once saw my parents kiss. Not once. I, on the other hand, was a very affectionate child. I loved cuddling with Mommy every morning, feeling her physical abundance embrace me. She'd tickle my ribs and nuzzle her nose in my neck like a warm puppy. I hated to leave her and get ready for school, preferring to stay home and listen to soap operas like "Stella Dallas" and "Grand Central Station."

I was eight when something happened that would forever change my world. This particular morning, as we snuggled and nuzzled, her hand wandered down to my "private place." I let her touch me there for maybe five or ten seconds, and then I jumped out of bed and raced down the hall to my own room. What she did felt good but somehow wrong. Very wrong. I never went in and snuggled with Mommy again.

Ever.

I never even kissed her.

It took a few years before I could come right out and ask her about what had happened that morning.

"You needed it," was all she said.

I needed it? What did she mean by that? I was only eight years old, for chrissake.

"You needed it," she repeated and then walked out of the room.

As a recovering alcoholic, I now know that blaming others is something alcoholics do on a regular basis. I also know that child molesters and rapists often accuse their victims of leading them on, encouraging them to act on their sexual desires. It took me years, but I eventually forgave my mother. She had a disease that she refused to acknowledge. And even if she had, the fellowship of Alcoholics Anonymous was something she knew nothing about.

...

I find love addiction expert Pia Mellody's writing on parental neglect or enmeshment fascinating. Much of what she writes strikes a familiar chord. In Leo's case, his mother's enmeshment created a *love avoidance* in him, whereas my mother's neglect (as a loving adult) set up a *love addiction* in me. In a checklist Pia Mellody titles "What a child learns from neglect and abandonment," I relate strongly to three of them:

• In adult relationships, this person will believe he/she cannot make it alone and needs someone to care for them.
• This person will also associate any distancing on the part of the partner (or friend, etc.) as a threat to his/her survival.
• All relationships become fear-based as well as shame-based.

In Leo's case, Mellody's checklist for "What a child learns from enmeshment" also rings true.

• This person will need to create a lot of intensity outside of the relationship.
• They create intensity to feel alive as opposed to the deadness that they feel in relationships.
• They can become antagonistic and aggressive both inside and outside of relationships, especially if they were "scapegoated."

*Which parent am I trying to replicate?*

My mother. And since a person's mother is usually the first love they experience, neither Leo's nor mine did us any favors. He still has trust issues around women; I have abandonment issues that make me want to trust the wrong people. Will my awareness of these things protect me from getting hurt again? Disillusioned? Or even abandoned? Hardly. Still, I'd rather risk it than give up trying for a happily-ever-after ending.

# CHAPTER ELEVEN

## Are old patterns resurfacing?

Leo and I have been together a little over a year.
Living in two different places — Vancouver and Sedona —
has definitely tested our emotional mettle. I've tried not to
pressure him about when he plans to come down here, but
reining in my impatience is getting more and more difficult. I
can't use our real estate investment as an excuse anymore. The
deal fell through. Disappointing as that news was, other things
are beginning to make me nervous.

### Red Flag #1

As I've already mentioned, Leo and I call each other
every morning at six o'clock to share our meditation books.
He uses one called "Touchstones: A Book of Daily Meditations
For Men" and I'm currently working with "Meditations for
Living in Balance" by Anne Wilson Schaff. Whether we're
in the same physical location or speaking by phone, trading
personal insights keeps our relationship honest and headed in
the right direction. We usually begin by reciting a few well-
chosen prayers. Here's Leo's favorite:

> *Look to this day!*
> *For it is life, the very life of life.*
> *In its brief course*
> *Lie all the verities*
> *and realities of existence:*
> *The bliss of growth;*
> *The glory of action;*
> *The splendor of achievement.*
> *For yesterday is but a dream.*
> *And tomorrow is only a vision;*

*But today, well lived, makes every yesterday*
*a dream of happiness*
*And every tomorrow a vision of hope.*
*Look well, therefore, to this day!*
Kalidasa

After we finish sharing, Leo mentions something about
looking forward to jamming with his former band mates that
afternoon. I'm all for him pursuing music. He's a talented
guy and wailing away on that Dobro gives him a chance to
vent any pent-up feelings he would otherwise stuff. But as we
talk about this jam session, I realize it isn't the first time these
guys have gotten together. They've been doing it every Friday
afternoon for a month.

A wave of panic washes over me.

We share everything. Why hasn't he said anything
about this? When I ask him, he hesitates, deciding whether to
lie or tell the truth. "I thought I did."

I wait for more information.

"Keith has a recording studio and we'll probably lay
down some tracks for three of my songs."

I say nothing.

"I just want a couple of demos for when I'm in Sedona
trying to get gigs."

Sounds reasonable enough. His former band mates,
Keith and Ted, are both married, drug-free and not alcoholics.

How threatening can that be?

"Well, have a good session," I say, exuding unfelt
enthusiasm. "I love you!"

"I love you, too."

After we hang up, I stare at the phone. It stares back at
me, cold and silent.

Every Friday afternoon, Leo continues jamming with
his former band mates. The more he tells me about these
sessions, the clearer it becomes that he hasn't told them
he's moving to Arizona. No longer able to contain myself, I
confront him about this. With no hesitation whatsoever, he
replies, "If I tell them I'm leaving, they'll drop me." My first
instinct is to reassure him that his former band mates would
never do that. Instead, I say nothing.

"I suppose you're right," he continues, answering my unspoken concern. "I should tell them. I know I should. Soon, I promise."

When we hang up, I don't feel the least bit reassured.

Two weeks later, it's my turn to get on a plane and head north. Leo says he can't wait to see me. "I even cancelled this week's jam session." I thank him, slightly annoyed that he feels compelled to tell me about it. ( I'm even more annoyed at myself for thanking him.)

After we've been together a couple of days, I ask him about his musician friends. Leo claims Keith is the only real pro. Ted sucks. "But he's the one who got us back together," Leo explains, barging ahead without thinking. "Revival bands are hot these days and Ted's convinced that, with enough rehearsing, we can land some paying gigs."

Suddenly, the room goes quiet.

"You haven't told them yet."

Leo looks down at his feet. "I don't feel good about this."

He openly admits that until he leaves town, he's just using these guys for his own musical amusement. I secretly wonder if he's using me for his own amusement, too.

"Next session, I'll tell them," he says. "You've got my word on that."

I nod tentatively, promising myself not to bring it up again.

### Red Flag #2

"I signed up for it before we got back together." Leo hands me a brochure with the description of a Wednesday night seminar titled: "A Woman's Erogenous Zones." I didn't care, really. If watching some sexologist stimulate his assistant's vulva turned Leo on, so be it.

It reminded me of a time after our fifth breakup when Leo registered for a course in massage. He was hoping it would improve his "technique" and possibly win me back. As I recall, his massages did improve. Later, he confessed that one of his assignments was to massage a naked lady's chest without touching her nipples. He'd failed that part.

After this latest sex seminar, Leo couldn't wait to expound on how neur ologically complicated a woman's labia majora and minora are. Not to mention the vestibule of the vagina. I heave a sigh of resignation. Does this mean his libido has returned in full force?

He assures I have nothing to worry about.

**Red Flag #3**

Leo grew up in the Psychedelic Sixties. Having fled to Canada to avoid the draft, he held any and all authority figures in contempt. As a boss, he was a pretty decent guy. Even when his various secretaries had to deal with irate customers because Leo had been drinking and forgot to show up, they gave him the benefit of the doubt. And he gave them generous Christmas bonuses.

Generous or not, he hated big government.

When he finally got serious about selling his business, no broker wanted it. The figures on his last five years of financial statements were misrepresented. I was aware of his flaky accountant's faulty bookkeeping but knew, if I mentioned anything, he'd shoot me down claiming I didn't know what I was talking about.

Now, however, his tax problem had become "our" tax problem.

I finally persuaded him to see my accountant. A straight-arrow type with thick horn rimmed glasses and even thicker suspenders. Maybe he could figure out a way to prevent Leo from winding up in a Canadian prison for tax evasion.

"I wouldn't advise redoing them," he told Leo, after scanning the last three years of his tax returns. "If you do, you'll only be bringing attention to the fact that these figures are irregular. They'll audit you for sure."

That wasn't the answer I was hoping for.

Still, the tax guys hadn't caught up with Leo yet. Maybe they never would. Another three months went by before he could accept the idea that nobody was going to purchase a business without proper tax documentation. He couldn't even get anyone to pay for his client lists. It was all

I could do not to blurt out, "If you'd paid your fucking taxes, none of this would be happening!"

Another expression I've learned in sobriety comes to mind: "*If you point a finger at someone else, three fingers are pointing back at you.*"

Would I pay taxes if I could get away without paying them? (No.)

When the IRS sends me a tax refund that seems too high, do I question it's validity? (No.)

If I saw a hundred dollar bill lying on the sidewalk, would I try and find its rightful owner? (Absolutely not.)

Leo eventually sold the business to a former employee, an impoverished gal who knew how to clean windows and dryer vents but didn't have a clue how to run an office. She agreed to give him a percentage of her earnings until he'd been paid back his asking price. Whether he ever sees a dime of that money isn't the point. It's how devious he still is. Using his musician friends. Registering for a sex course when he claims he's not that interested. Under paying his taxes and thereby sabotaging the sale of his own business. Is this really someone I want to spend the rest of my life with?

...

Codependency is one of those terms that's been defined in so many different ways that it's lost much of its value. In a nutshell, it refers to someone who has become so preoccupied and focused on the needs of another person, they completely neglect their own needs. Leo obviously hasn't neglected his own needs in certain areas. Nor have I. However, we do fit the definition offered by authors Cathleen Clements and Barbara Bofenkamp, who describe a codependent as, "One whose dependency needs were not met during early developmental stages, who is continually seeking validation of self worth, and who attempts to recreate the parent/child relationships in other significant relationships."

Neither of our dependency needs were met in early childhood — at least not in healthy ways. His Momma loved him too much. Mine, too little. We are both aware of our codependency on each other and are working on not letting the other person's problems engulf us. I have to keep reminding myself that Leo is only a year and three months sober.

*Are old patterns resurfacing?*

I'm not sure. What I am sure of is, we are dealing more directly with these issues than we ever have before. Leo is motivated to be more truthful these days. So what if he had a "slip" and wasn't honest with his former band mates. He did tell them before he left. As far as I'm concerned, the jury is still out on whether Leo's destructive patterns are too firmly entrenched to change. It will take more time — and more bad decisions on his part — before I sentence the relationship to death. I prefer focusing on today rather than fretting about what's past or what's ahead. Like Kalidasa's prayer advises, *"Today, well-lived, makes every yesterday a dream of happiness and every tomorrow a vision of hope."*

# CHAPTER TWELVE

## Is a new project the answer?

Funny how problems often get solved in unexpected ways. Someone shows up on your doorstep just when you need them. A surprise check arrives in the mail when you thought you wouldn't be able to pay this month's phone bill. The answer to my insecurities about Leo came in the form of a two-bedroom foreclosure that was too good to pass up. Once the short sale had fallen through, neither of us wanted to stop shopping for real estate. Only now we planned to live there ourselves. For a second time, we made a ridiculously low offer. The bank accepted it within twenty-four hours.

Suddenly a new project had materialized.

Despite the rather ominous address — "Devil's Canyon" — the place was everything Leo and I could have asked for. Spacious living room, cathedral ceilings, lots of storage space and privacy. There was even enough room on the back patio to install a hot tub. With Leo still living in Vancouver, renovating our jointly purchased condo became a welcome distraction. No longer was I obsessing over his band mates or his unpaid tax bill, I was too busy picking pavers and paint colors.

The second bedroom had five walls so Leo christened it The Goofy Room. We gave each wall a different color — tan, green, terra cotta. Believe it or not, the effect was enchanting. Leo and I both love Navajo designs but once I saw how pricy those hand-woven rugs were, I decided to paint the actual designs directly on our walls.

"You could have a whole new career," an artist friend told me.

"Don't have time."

"Then make time!" he insisted.

I was extremely flattered by Hal's endorsement of my artistic talent. Through the years, being creative has always been my salvation.

### Miss Madeira's – Late 1950's

I was a rebellious teenager. Boys were my main interest, not good grades. That unwelcome phrase, "She could do better if she applied herself" became every teacher's appraisal of me. In sharp contrast, my sister was brainy and well-behaved. If she wanted to be "Goodie Two Shoes," let her. I had other ways of getting attention.

Like playing hookey from school one day, stealing my mom's Studebaker and driving down to The Brooklyn Naval Yard to surprise my boyfriend Gerry. I cajoled two other classmates into joining me. Gerry was shocked. And so was the headmistress when she discovered three of her girls were absent from class that day. She suspended me for two weeks, advising my parents that it might be a wise idea to send me away to boarding school. Clearly, living at home wasn't giving me the academic structure or discipline I needed.

I begged. I pleaded. I made all sorts of promises but my dad remained resolute. The boarding school he chose was in Fairfax County, Virginia. It had an excellent reputation, a lovely campus and the best riding stables in the country. To me, it was just a high-priced prison. How was I ever going to survive in an all girls' school?

"You could write a musical!" I stared at my sister in disbelief. "You're always making up songs, inventing new harmonies. I bet if you wrote a musical, the time would pass a lot quicker."

"I can't. I'll be too depressed."

"All I'm saying is—"

"Forget it!" I was mad at myself for asking her opinion in the first place.

On the train ride down to Virginia, oak trees and tenements whirring by in a blur, I kept thinking about the musical I wasn't going to write. About this poor waif of a girl whose parents shipped her off to boarding school, where she fell in love with a black stable hand and they eloped together never to be heard from again!

I wondered if any of those horsey types could sing.

It turned out they could. And dance. And write. Before the month was up, I went to the dean and suggested our class put together a talent show. That talent show morphed into "Soph Party" for which I wrote the songs and Buffy Beardsley scripted and directed the skits. It was such a success that each year since the sophomore class puts on a show for the rest of the student body.

By June, I'd convinced my dad that I was ready to come home and behave properly. My grades had improved and so had my attitude. More important than boys, or breaking rules, music had become the life preserver I needed to stay afloat.

### Lake Arrowhead, California – Mid 80's

What makes a writer good is the ability to be both creative and self-critical. When I reread a poem I've penned, or an article, or a short story, I immediately see what's wrong with it rather than what's right. "It was a dark and stormy night" written by Victorian novelist Edward Bulwer-Lytton has become the ultimate example of purple prose. Overly dramatic or not, I'll bet Baron Bulwer-Lytton toiled over whether to use "dank" instead of "dark," " rain-spattered" instead of "stormy." Writers are a fussy bunch, never completely happy with what they've written.

There was a point in my career where I was so tired of being my own worst critic that I decided to pack it in and become a house painter. I wanted instant gratification for a change. (Of course the real reason had more to do with the heroin addict I was living with. Remember him? )

We both felt Dee's self-esteem would benefit from having a steady job. When I asked him what gave him the most pleasure, he replied, "Painting houses." So that's what we did. I learned the tricks of the trade: how to clean brushes, the advantages of latex versus oil-based paints, which scrapers to use. Only problem was, my partner was afraid of heights. Considering how much time he'd spent in the joint, I found this hilarious. Fearing heights seemed like small potatoes compared to the threat of losing one's life over a pack of smokes. Still, I didn't mind scampering up and down those rungs like a mountain-monkey.

Dee would make the initial contact, bid on the job, buy the supplies and work his ass off prepping the exteriors. By the third day, he'd disappear. There I'd be, surrounded by buckets of paint and freshly laid tarps, telling myself that he was just off buying more supplies. He'd be back in fifteen minutes. But those fifteen minutes would turn into days, even weeks. The pop music group *Genesis* was big at the time and I remember thinking, as Phil Collins belted out "That's All," how appropriate those lyrics were:

> *Just as I thought it was going alright*
> *I find out I'm wrong, when I thought I was right*
> *s'always the same, it's just a shame, that's all*

I cringed inwardly at:

> *Turning me on, turning me off,*
> *making me feel like I want too much*
> *living with you's just putting me through it*
> *all of the time*
> *running around, staying out all night*
> *taking it all instead of taking one bite*
> *living with you's just putting me through it all of the time**

Needless to say, I got a great deal of satisfaction from transforming some weather beaten A-frame into a sparkling jewel, freshly painted and pristine. I'd stand back admiring the trim, how each line had been carefully cut. My sense of accomplishment was immediate — and I could find nothing to criticize. Unlike the men I've chosen to love, my creativity has never let me down.

## Summer - 1999

I met Clark at a writers' group. He was sexy, in a
boyish sort of way, but too young for me. May-December
romances (especially when you're December) aren't my thing.
The idea that someone might mistake me for my boyfriend's
mother is an insult I never want to experience. Still, Clark and I
shared a mutual love of words.

His particular passion was poetry.

In high school, I'd been forced to memorize Samuel
Taylor Coleridge's "Kubla Kahn" (" *In Xanadu did Kubla Khan
A stately pleasure-dome decree...*" ) along with Chaucer's "*When
that Aprile with his shoures soote...*" With no prompting from
Miss Jerrold, our English teacher, I also memorized Vachel
Lindsay's "The Congo" because I loved the way the words had
a jungle rhythm all their own. (" *Fat black bucks in a wine-barrel
room, Barrel-house kings, with feet unstable, Sagged and reeled and
pounded on the table...*" ) Later on in college, I memorized Emily
Dickinson's "*My candle burns at both ends*" because it made me
sound sophisticated and complemented the image I was trying
to project—smoking Chesterfield Kings in an ivory cigarette
holder and tossing off bittersweet one-liners.

One evening after Clark had finished reading me Walt
Whitman's "Song of Myself," he produced a certificate of
merit from a poetry writing contest. He'd won four hundred
dollars. I was blown away and wondered how different
sonnet-writing would be from songwriting. As Clark and I
became more emotionally enmeshed, I discovered he was
as hooked on pot as he was on poetry. In spite of his two
previous marriages, I also thought he was gay.

We became lovers anyway.

I tried valiantly to ignore his exaggerated hand
gestures, high-pitched giggle, unmanly hip movements. But
my homosexual suspicions never wavered. In the end his love
affair with weed, combined with his womanly ways, made
me back off. Still, I'm grateful for the six months I spent with
Clark. By reacquainting me with Wordsworth's "I Wandered
Lonely As A Cloud" and Ginsberg's "Howl," he rekindled my
infatuation with words and writing formal poetry became a
whole new avenue of expression. I had no desire to jump into

bed with the next warm body I could find. Instead, I wrote sonnets, basking in the beauty of iambic pentameter.

...

Author Eric Hoffer put it best when he wrote, "Creativity is discontent translated into arts." Composing songs, painting houses, writing sonnets has helped me work through periods of my own discontent. These accomplishments have given me a sense of control over my life, albeit a temporary one. Unfortunately, they haven't erased my need to be with a man. And he's not always a nice man, either. That's the downside of being creative. You can make princes out of pricks. I honestly don't think I'm doing that with Leo. He has made mistakes in the past, but then so have I.

*Is a new project the answer?*

How many couples think a baby will save their marriage? Or moving to a different part of the country? Even having an extra marital affair. Sometimes these things actually strengthen a relationship. Everyone's needs are different. My need right now is to believe, with all my heart, that Leo and I have a real chance at happiness. My left brain might argue, "You've already had more than enough chances and they always fall apart in the end." Then my right brain pipes up with, "Look at the changes you've both made over the past year. Give yourself credit and don't give up now!" Something as seemingly simple as refurbishing a foreclosure has infused our relationship with new energy and a new purpose in life.

# PART THREE – RESOLUTION

Resolve to be thyself; and know that he,
Who finds himself, loses his misery.

– Matthew Arnold -

# CHAPTER THIRTEEN

## Why do I still have doubts?

They say the opposite of doubt is faith. I never was much of a bible-thumper, preferring to quote Karl Marx whenever I could. (" *Religion is the opiate of the masses.* " ) Then I got sober and it forced me to take another look at faith. And God. "*Fake it till you make it,*" my fellow sobriety-seekers told me. I must admit believing in a power greater than myself has been a real comfort. Especially when I've felt helpless and hopeless.

I don't mean to sound like Chicken Little as far as my relationship with Leo is concerned. The sky is definitely not falling in right now. If anything, it's a perfect blue with nary a cirrus cloud in sight. Still, late at night when I hear the coyotes yipping in the distance, I begin to question whether Leo and I are making another tragic mistake.

"Everything'll be fine," I quickly reassure myself. "You both have a beautiful home. He's sold his condo. You love each other."

Sometimes these pep talks do the trick. At other times, it's as if those yipping coyotes are warning me to "Get out before it's too late!" That's when prayer helps. I don't ask God to do anything anymore. I did that decades ago at Christ Church Cathedral, when I asked Him to make my mother stop drinking. Now when I pray it's about having faith, trusting that my Higher Power knows what I need more than I do. When I pray long and hard enough, the coyotes go quiet.

### Messages From Beyond – 1992

When Dee died he had two funerals. One in Riverside, California and the other in Grants Pass, Oregon. I attended both. After the doctors told him he had terminal cancer, he came back to LA and lived with me. I took him to his chemotherapy sessions, rented all the Pink Panther movies so we could laugh together. I even got him a plant. I'm no gardener so I can't tell you whether it was honeysuckle or hibiscus. All I know is, he'd sit out on the balcony for hours at a time, smoking his Pall Malls and watching it grow. Willing it to grow, actually. As if by seeing another living thing thrive, he'd regain his own health. Cancer treatments weren't as advanced as they are today. Dee suffered horribly. Blisters on the inside of his mouth, food tasting metallic, weight loss that made him avoid looking in mirrors. He dreaded taking showers, fearing that if he fell in the tub he'd break every fragile bone in his body.

In spite of all this, I was amazed how upbeat he seemed.

We attended a clinic in Santa Monica for cancer patients and their caregivers. It gave us both a chance to air our grievances without the other one knowing. We caregivers were obsessed with feeding our loved ones, hoping food would make them get better. According to Dee, the cancer patients would complain about their mates trying to make them eat when they didn't feel like eating. They also felt guilty about dying, leaving loved ones to cope on their own.

I was with Dee when he died. The oxygen machine stopped beeping at three-thirty in the morning just as his mother came bursting in the room. She knew intuitively that her son had met his Maker. I drove back to LA to get a change of clothes and cry in private. A friend came over, a guy who knew all there was to know about plants.

"Why is that dead honeysuckle out on your balcony?" he asked.

I replied, "It wasn't dead the last time I looked."

"Well it is now."

Brown sticks jutted out from a cracked flowerpot. Remembering how green and lush Dee's plant once was, I added weakly, "Maybe it just needs watering."

"You should have thought of that weeks ago, hon."

"I'll throw it away when I get back from Oregon," I told him.

By the time Dee had his second funeral, his body

had begun shrinking. In life, he was six feet tall. In death, he looked like an unhappy leprechaun in an ill-fitting suit. To make matters worse, his make-up was overdone.

Diesel would have hated the way he looked.

I'm back in LA now. Slowly getting used to the idea that I'll never feel his presence in my life again. I'd made some friends at the clinic. Ladies mostly, whose husbands had either died already, or were well on their way. Their phone calls and sympathy meant everything to me. I wasn't quite ready to get on with the business of living and neither were they. These people knew Dee, saying his name didn't make them squirm like my other friends.

One day, I remembered Dee's plant. It was time for me to toss it down the garbage chute. When I went outside on the balcony, I had to catch my breath. There it was. In full bloom. How was that possible? My gardener friend had said the plant was definitely dead. Well, it wasn't anymore!

After that, I renamed it Dee. His kids loved that their dad had a permanent place on my balcony. I am the furthest thing from a woo-woo type despite living in Sedona. But I have no rational explanation for why that dead plant suddenly came alive again.

A lot of other caregivers had similar stories. This one Jewish lady (whose religion didn't include the concept of an afterlife) said that her husband, before he died, jokingly told her he'd come back as a bird. A few days after his funeral, a robin flew in through the kitchen window, circled the living room once and then fluttered away. It had never happened before. Nor has it happened since.

Another fellow told me about a dying friend who suddenly sat up just before he died, looked straight ahead as if he recognized somebody across the room, and cried, "Dad!" I don't have an answer for why these otherworldly events take place. I do know Dee was a great talker and perhaps the blooming plant was his way of not being silenced.

If I had to choose which I'm more in doubt about, an afterlife, or my relationship with Leo, I'd definitely pick the former. Whether it's true or not, I feel I have some control over my current reality. As for after I die? I don't have a clue. Although Haley Joel Osment's line "I see dead people" in *The*

*Sixth Sense* became a classic, nothing like that has ever been my experience. I have, however, witnessed couples whose bad relationships have ultimately turned around. Some of it has to do with changes in their behavior. But a lot has to do with them having faith in the relationship itself.

*Why do I still have doubts?*

Growing up as I did with an alcoholic mother who reenforced my fears on a daily basis, it's only natural for me to have my doubts. About Leo, about our relationship. But mostly about me. Will I somehow screw it up? Will my impatience be my undoing? My AA sponsor always encourages me to voice these apprehensions. "Name it, claim it and dump it!" she advises.

Easier said than done," I think to myself.

Then my optimism kicks in. I'll silence any leftover fears by thinking about something positive — an Arizona sunset, the smell of pine cones, a friend from childhood.

We all have doubts.

Why should I be any different?

# CHAPTER FOURTEEN

## What happens now?

I'm really excited. Leo is coming down for a month this time, his last visit before moving here permanently. We can share our morning meditations in front of a crackling fire, warm up the bed together every night. I can't wait to play silly games, make corny puns, beat him at gin rummy. We've got lots of social events planned, including my annual Oscar party and the Sedona International Film Festival. I also can't wait to show him the progress on our condo. Now he'll be here to help me decide which plants to get for the patio, what color to stain the fence. I don't feel comfortable making all these decisions on my own.

A lot has happened in Leo's absence.

I had a lumpectomy on my right breast. It turned out to be benign but it hurt like hell — and fearing that it might be cancer, hurt even more. The same girlfriend from Winnipeg was with me at the time so I was in capable and caring hands.

It would've been nicer if those hands had been Leo's.

Two weeks later, my cat stopped eating. No matter how much I tried to coax her, she refused. Her weight loss was dramatic. Within forty-eight hours, her cougar-round face had turned skeletal. Too weak to jump up on my bed, she wouldn't stop trying. Those questioning eyes drove a stake through my heart. I knew she was dying but couldn't face it. Finally, I drove her up to the emergency animal clinic in Flagstaff. The vet took blood samples and administered fluids intravenously. When she returned with the test results, she confirmed my own unhappy suspicions. "If you hadn't brought that cat in when you did, she wouldn't have survived the night."

This turned out to be of little consolation since she also said my cat's kidneys had failed and her death was inevitable. I was faced with the dreaded decision so many pet owners are forced to make. Do I put my constant companion of fifteen years to sleep? Or do I let her die a natural and unnecessarily painful death.

Leo tried to be supportive but in the end it was my decision. My friend Robin's cat had recently died and she suggested I ask the vet to come to the condo to put mine down. I took her advice and was glad I did. It made Beauty's final moments far less frightening. As I sobbed into my pillow that night, I missed Leo terribly. The sound of his snoring would have been preferable to the haunting silence that permeated the room, reminding me that this loving creature would never again curl up in my arms.

### Valentine's Day - 2009

Now that Leo has arrived, his arms are the ones I curl up in. Today we're planning to celebrate this special day by going to a local bistro, long stemmed roses on every table. The jazz singer's mellow rendition of "The Girl From Ipanema" is making everybody in the room feel more romantic. Who'd have predicted such a perfect ending for us two years ago?

The Saint Valentine's Day Massacre was the name given to the murder of seven people gunned down in Chicago in 1929 on Valentine's Day. The massacre that took place two days after our heartfelt celebration didn't involve killing anyone. It did, however, snuff out any feelings of love I had for Leo.

We're at my rented condo and I'm helping him clear out his old emails. Despite numerous computer classes, the poor guy is still a novice when it comes to navigating the internet. While deleting his correspondence, I notice a Christmas card he sent one of his computer classmates named Sonja. According to Leo, she's been trying unsuccessfully to quit drinking. He's even taken her to several AA meetings in an attempt to follow the suggestion offered in Step Twelve about *"carrying the message to other alcoholics who are still suffering."*

"Want me to delete this Christmas card to Sonja? "

"Sure."

I forget what happens next. Maybe I go grocery

shopping, or I wash my hair. It doesn't matter. What matters is that Leo remains in the living room, a chair away from my laptop. When I return a few hours later to check my own email messages, I notice one he has just sent to Sonja. The subject line reads: "Lonesome Leo.

"What's this? " I ask.

"What's what? "

"Lonesome Leo."

Without a moment's hesitation he confesses that he sent Sonja a flirtatious email, praying for a little action when he returned to Vancouver. "It was a stupid thing to do," he admits, unable or unwilling to look me in the eye. "But I have a lot of fear going on in me right now. About retiring, getting older, coming down here and living with you. We both know you don't really enjoy sex. Sure, you're a good sport about it. But I wanted to have one last fling."

I stare at him, not knowing how to respond.

"She turned me down flat," he adds. "Wanna read her reply? "

"Not really."

I stumble out of the room, dizzy with disbelief. This cannot be happening. I've put so much time and energy into this relationship, not to mention love. What do I do now? Kick him out? Keep him here? Leo has been unfaithful to other women but never to me. In fact, he often brings up my infidelities. From his perspective, we're still a couple whether we're together or not.

I say that's ridiculous. Whenever we've split up, I'm instantly on the lookout for a new man to ease my pain. Leo eases his pain with the other love of his life: booze. Sometimes he'll bed down with Jack Daniels. At other times, Merlot. During this last bout, when he nearly committed suicide, he was intimately involved with Saki.

After accidentally discovering his email to Sonja, part of me wants him out of my sight. If he's so hell-bent on having one last fling, let him go back to Canada and have it. (I hope he gets AIDS.)

Then the realization hits me.

How will I live without Leo in my life?

My emotions seesaw back and forth between hurt, hate

and need. Some love addicts are more eager and willing to forgive than others. That's not my style. But what about the Oscar party? The film festival? How do I explain his sudden departure to all my friends? Maybe, if we share these things, I'll be able to forget.

"I wanted to get caught," Leo argues. "Otherwise, why would I use *your* laptop? "

Whatever his excuse—self-sabotage, insensitivity, male ego—I don't care. My shoulders shake uncontrollably, as I finally let my grief out of its cage. "You've destroyed our dream, Leo. I can no longer trust you. Ever."

. . .

The journalist in me wants to rush right out and ask other women (and men) how they've handled an unfaithful spouse or lover. Were they able to forgive them? I suddenly remember a show on TV about cheaters. "Over eighty percent of husbands who cheat on their wives will do it again," a well-known doctor tells his audience. Am I capable of dismissing Leo's libidinal impulses? None of my other lovers have played around on me. Not unless you count Fernando Montez de Oca.

### Vaya Con Dios - 1968

This story begins in Mexico City when I was twenty-four. I went there on vacation, planning to stay two weeks and ended up living there for two years. I met Fernando on the steps of the city's most important cultural center, the *Palacio De Bellas Artes*, where he worked as a tour guide. Dressed in a navy blue uniform with gold epaulets, Fernando was striking-looking in an Aztec sort of way. He had high cheekbones, obsidian eyes and an irresistible grin. He was different than any man I'd ever dated, favoring socialism over democracy and hanging out with a bunch of avowed communists.

Naturally, this was a turn-on to me.

I was also turned on by living in a foreign land where nobody knew anything about me, other than the fact that I was an American. Renting a room off *Avenida Paseo de la Reforma*

(Mexico City's Fifth Avenue equivalent), I earned my keep by teaching English to insurance agents and playing guitar at *La Rana Sabia* (The Wise Frog). Fernando professed his undying love for me, but I knew it would never last.

After a year and a half of rough toilet paper, movies dubbed in Spanish and beggars on every street corner — mostly children, egged on by their parents — I decided I'd had enough foreignness for awhile. As we embraced at the Benito Juárez International Airport, I promised to write every day.

When I returned to New York, I moved in with my mother. My parents had divorced and, as part of the settlement, she lived in a roomy penthouse on West Eighty-Sixth Street. A block away was a neighborhood pub, "The Tip Toe Inn," where she spent many inebriated hours jawing with the likes of Hal Holbrook and (according to her, anyway) Gail Sheehy. It was a challenge sharing space together. I never knew from one minute to the next who I'd be spending time with. The funny, self-deprecating mom who made me laugh? Or the bitterly critical woman who loathed her ex-husband.

As Christmas approached, I asked my father if we could invite Fernando to West Hartford for the holidays. Considering how hospitable he'd been to me during my stay in his country, it was the least we could do. As usual, I was broke so Daddy paid for the airline ticket.

Fernando had never seen snow, tasted oatmeal, or been so showered with Christmas gifts in his life. I loved showing him off to my conservative friends and relations. He wasn't terribly Mexican-looking but his broken English gave him away. The rebel in me secretly smirked at their muted reactions. I wasn't about to settle down with some Ivy Leaguer, have two and a half kids, drive a Ford station wagon and become one more unhappily married statistic.

When Christmas was over, we went back to live with my mother. Fernando was bowled over by the city's towering skyscrapers, Broadway's hustle-bustle, the various ethnic types pouring in and out of every subway station. He would've given anything to marry me and remain here forever.

That was never going to happen.

When my mother drank, she often got overly

flirtatious. Poor Fernando would fend off her bourbon-soaked kisses as best he could. But eventually he and I had to move. Having gotten a refund for his return trip ticket to Mexico City, we lived off that money until it ran out. Then we took turns selling blood to pay for our scuzzy hotel room. The kinkiness of this kind of poverty soon wore thin. So did Fernando's political rants about the benefits of socialism over democracy.

"He's driving me crazy!" I steeled myself for a lecture, knowing my father would ultimately buy Fernando another plane ticket back to Mexico City. "Please, Daddy! You have to get rid of him for me!" Only too happy to oblige, my father phoned his travel agent.

Fernando was hurt but he didn't try to dissuade me. He just nodded his head, accepting his fate with grace and stoicism. When I offered to wait with him at JFK, he said that wouldn't be necessary.

"*Vaya con Dios!*" I shouted, as I pulled away from the curb.

"*Y tu tambièn,*" he responded, an odd grin lighting up his classic Aztec face.

I lived with my dad for the next three months. The price I was expected to pay for his grand gesture of generosity. When I returned to Manhattan, I moved into a darling apartment on Third Avenue and began working as a receptionist at Pan Am. After I'd settled in, I invited my mother over to see the place. She was uncharacteristically vague about her plans. And so, by my third unanswered phone message, I decided to pay her a surprise visit.

It was a surprise all right.

When I rang her bell, Fernando opened the door. He'd cashed in his airline ticket and moved in with my mother. I didn't bother asking if they were sharing the same bed. Either way, I felt screwed. Not so much by Fernando. He would definitely improve his life by living in the states. It was my mother I felt betrayed by. Here she was, sheltering my ex-boyfriend and hiding it from her own daughter.

*You never can tell, Mommy. You never can tell. . . .*

...

Still obsessed with trying to find out how other couples cope with infidelity, I type "Cheating Husbands" in Yahoo's search window. The first site that pops up on screen tells me: "Fifty percent of all men will cheat on their wives at some point." Not much comfort there. As I scroll down further, another statement really makes my blood boil. "Husbands are more likely to feel that cheating is justified due to the lack of sex within a marriage." Unlike many women who are in long-term relationships, I have never withheld affection from Leo. Nor have I denied him access to my body. The ways in which we pleasure each other may have changed through the years, but the willingness hasn't.

I suddenly remember a married woman I know whose husband cheated on her. When I phone, asking how she managed to repair their relationship, she doesn't want to talk about it. "What's past is past," she tells me. Undeterred, I query the only man I know whose wife was unfaithful to him. His answer? "I forgave her. What choice did I have?"

*What happens now?*

I'm reminded of a quote by Oscar Wilde: *"When one is in love, one always begins by deceiving one's self, and one always ends by deceiving others."* At this point, my wounds are still too fresh to think about forgiving Leo. I want nothing more to do with that selfish bastard. No more emails, no more phone calls. And certainly no more phony meditations. In the past, my resolve has usually crumbled. I get too lonely and too scared about my future. Right now I need to surround myself with friends who know what to say to make me feel better. I have to keep busy. Lots of Al-Anon meetings, lots of tennis. In a month or two, maybe, I'll stop beating myself up with, "Why didn't you see this coming?" Years back, I would've immediately gone out and screwed some other guy. (Remember Carson and his blind cat Zoey?) Today, I'm thinking more along the lines of some good revenge companionship.

# CHAPTER FIFTEEN

## Where do we go from here?

As a professional songwriter, I can appreciate how difficult it is to come up with a phrase or title that says so much in so few words. The Bee Gees' "How Can You Mend A Broken Heart?" accomplishes that brilliantly. Corny as those lyrics may seem to today's rappers, they capture how I'm feeling. I have about as much chance to *"stop the rain from falling"* or *"the sun from shining"* as I do forgetting Leo's adulterous email. Even if Sonja did turn him down, what happens when the next one doesn't?

And there will be a next one.

Like a lingering cold, the days drag on without relief. I know I must stay strong but I miss our silly little games, hearing him practice guitar, the feeling of togetherness. Besides, I am somewhat responsible for him selling his condo, his business, leaving his kids to move down here. It's been a month since Leo returned to Canada. At my insistence, we've had zero contact. I'm ready now to extend the first long distance olive branch. Punching in his phone number, I try to contain my fear — and my excitement.

"Hi, Leo."

"Hi."

Neither one of us knows what to say next. Too much silence always makes me uncomfortable so I blurt out the only question worth asking." Where do we go from here? "

Long pause.

"I'd like —" his voice is unsteady. He sounds nervous. "I'd like to reinstate our morning meditations." I can almost hear his heartbeat. "I realize it will take time before you can trust me. But I'm hoping someday you will."

"I'll try."

It's crazy, I know. Like pouring more money into a bad

stock, praying it will reverse itself. And sometimes it does. When we hang up, agreeing to phone at our usual time the next morning, a whoosh of relief washes over me. Darkness has been replaced by a paper thin sliver of light.

During that first week of contact, I discover an online article about rebuilding trust after an affair. Granted Leo's affair never came to pass but the intent was there. I email the article to him, asking that he comment on each point. The author offers eight suggestions:

#1. Stop lying.

#2. Do not get defensive or assign blame.

#3. Cut any and all possible ties with the other woman.

#4. Your life must be an open book.

#5. Be prepared to answer any and all questions about things that your spouse has a legitimate right to know.

#6. Do not attempt to dictate the length of time the victim spouse's recovery should take.

#7. Do not behave inappropriately or create future problems. Don't put yourself in situations which will cause your victim spouse undue stress.

#8. Finally, and most importantly, make sure you are truly ready to be faithful and committed to your marriage before attempting to rebuild trust. Nothing is more devastating to a victim spouse then learning to trust a person who betrays them again.

Number Three (cutting any and all possible ties) brings up some uncomfortable truths. According to Leo, he had lent Sonja his electric keyboard. This admission rankles, as he originally bought that keyboard for me. He's always had a thing for songbirds. One of his standard moves was to lend or even buy his latest romantic prey whatever musical instrument she fancied.

His email reads, "I have arranged for one of my workers to pick up the keyboard from Sonja. I want nothing more to do with her."

Leo addresses each point in detail, trying to prove—in heartfelt prose—how very sorry he is. When I read his reply to Number Seven (not putting yourself or your partner in situations which cause undue stress), I'm impressed with the sacrifices he's willing to make.

"I know playing in clubs is probably not a good idea right now." He's got that one right. "I wouldn't want to cause you any more pain than I already have." So far, so good. "My goal would be to make some demos and try to sell them to other recording artists. That way, you wouldn't have to worry about what I was doing or where I was going." It all sounds very logical and conciliatory. Then I read his last sentence and laugh out loud. "I won't even bring a guitar if it'll make you feel any better."

I know he's kidding about that and so does he.

Making me laugh and making me trust him again are two entirely different things. I appreciate how hard he is trying. Nonetheless, I have to protect myself the only way I know how. By reactivating my profile on Match.com and Plenty of Fish. This time I'm seeking new tennis partners. Men only, around my same age. "They're harder hitters than women," I tell myself. "I'll get a better workout that way."

Who am I kidding?

My quest isn't about tennis. It's about finding someone to *"help me mend my broken heart and let me live again."*

### Hal Epstein

I met two other tennis players before Hal Epstein (a pseudonym) came into my life. They were quirky guys who didn't attract me physically, but were eager to learn all they could about the game. I was the better player and fell easily into the role of instructor. Hal, on the other hand, was a far more accomplished athlete. Within minutes of our first rally, I gave him "The Bird" for hitting such an unreturnable shot. Would he be insulted? Amused? Whatever he felt didn't deter him from whacking more tennis balls beyond my reach.

He was a very attractive man. Especially his salt-and-pepper hair styled like Prince Valiant, a comic book hero who wore his hair in a pageboy. When Hal and I took a time out, I became even more intrigued. He'd been in the Peace Corps, spoke fluent Spanish. And he'd published two books—one on fund-raising, the other on finance. He'd worked on Wall Street, been a college professor, owned a men's clothing store. His marital track record, however, was less impressive.

Married twice for only one year each, he quickly explained
that his communication skills back then weren't good. He
assured me he was far more enlightened these days.

His store back east had gone belly up. At the invitation
of an artist friend, he'd come to Arizona and never left.
Borrowing the same friend's sculpting tools, Hal started
shaping and reshaping pieces of indigenous wood, turning
them into salable *object d'art*. To supplement his dwindling
income, he worked as a waiter at numerous establishments
around town. Too old now to remember people's orders or
cater to their demands, he rented out rooms in a rambling
old house in Cottonwood where he himself was a renter. The
extra income helped supplement his Social Security checks,
allowing him to buy more art supplies.

### Another Time, Another Tennis Court – Early 90's

I'm in LA. It's been three months since Dee's death and
I've enrolled in The K.I.S.S. Broadcasting Workshop, hoping
to become the next Barbara Walters. The school is in the heart
of Hollywood and, believe it or not, there's a tennis court atop
of one of the nearby office buildings. I see an ad: "Looking For
Tennis Partners. Call Ray at. . ."

When I phone Ray that evening, he has a thick French
accent. We agree to meet the next day and, as he strides
confidently across the tennis court, I am pleasantly surprised
by his Cary Grant good looks. Then I notice the wedding ring.
No, thank you. I didn't need any more disappointments in
my life right now. He wasn't great at tennis. He hit the ball
more like a badminton player, scooping it up from the ground
rather than hitting it at waist level. Still, he could beat me with
one hand tied behind his back.

One Wednesday, Ray announced that it was his
birthday. I insisted on treating him to a cup of coffee. It was
the first time we discussed anything other than tennis. He was
half-French, half-Lebanese. After a painful second divorce,
he'd left Canada hoping to make a fresh start in the United
States. In order to get a work permit — commonly known
as a green card — he'd married his landlady. Right now he
was working for a pest company spraying yards and killing

termites. Quite a comedown from his earlier career as a successful insurance agent for SunLife. I didn't press him any further on that subject. I did, however, ask for more details about his marriage-of-convenience.

"Ah, Lillian. She's a lonely old woman. I used to rent a room from her but when I told her my situation, how I'd have to go back to Canada if I didn't find someone to marry, she offered to marry me." I looked at him more closely. "There's nothing romantic between us," he continued. "It's strictly a business deal." It was his turn now to find out more about me.

"I recently lost someone I loved very much," I told him. "To cancer."

"I'm sorry for your loss."

Now we both knew where we stood. He didn't love his wife and my partner had just died. Soon we became much more than tennis buddies. When Ray moved in with me, his wife-of-convenience suddenly became hysterical. "But I love you, Raymond!" she cried. Then she started showing up at his place of employment, embarrassing him in front of his coworkers. Aside from being arrogantly French, Ray's Arab genes couldn't tolerate this woman's audacity. The very next day he went to city hall in Santa Monica and filed for divorce.

"Won't that jeopardize your status here? " I asked.

"Then I'll move back to Canada." He paused, suddenly remembering that I was now part of the equation. "You are most welcome to join me, if you wish."

The minute his divorce was final, Ray was told he had sixty days to leave the United States. Despite some obvious cultural and religious differences, I wasn't about to let my new love addiction go to Canada without me. Sure, there were things that bothered me about Ray. His crazy sister always ringing him up, begging him to save her from some new calamity. His sex toys. The fact that he actually moved all the stuff he had in storage from Burbank, California to some place in Nevada because he believed a prediction from Nostradamus that the world was coming to an end. But he made up for those faults by cooking exotic Middle Eastern dishes like *baba ganoush, humus, falafel*.

In light of my current situation, the most important thing about Ray was where he took me next. He landed a job

selling life insurance in Vancouver, British Columbia. When
all the company's leads turned into no sales, they let him
go. Next, he tried selling jewelry. He was no better at that. I
remember when my dad met him, he told me, "As long as he's
employed, he'll be fine. But if that man isn't working, he'll
make your life miserable." My dad was right, as usual. After
a year and a half of trying, Ray and I called it quits. Still, if we
hadn't met on that tennis court in Hollywood, I would never
have ended up in Vancouver — and this memoir would never
have been written.

...

Leo is scheduled to arrive in two weeks. I'm not sure
how I feel about this. It's rather like an annual checkup.
You either leave the doctor's office, relieved that you're still
healthy. Or you totter out in shock, having been told you've
got some incurable disease. I have no idea what the results
will be when we see each other again. One thing I am certain
about. Hal's company makes me feel wonderful. At seventy-
four he pretends to be an old grouch, but he's really a *mensch*.
He knows his movies, his music and how to help me edit the
book I'm working on. The more time we spend together, the
more time we want to spend together. Despite the obvious
sexual chemistry between us, I don't encourage it. That's Leo's
domain.

I wouldn't call what I'm doing with Hal rebounding.
There's still a part of me clinging to the notion that Leo and I
are soulmates, that in the final analysis we belong together. I
keep hoping my belief in a Higher Power will somehow make
it all better.

Speaking of miracles, reminds me of when I quit
drinking. I wasn't one of those falling down, booze-in-a-
paper-bag drunks. But I sure scarfed down plenty of red wine
on a daily basis. At one of my first AA meetings, I spoke up
and said I was afraid I'd never be able to give up drinking
completely. My craving for alcohol would eventually triumph.
A lady approached me afterward, suggesting I ask my Higher
Power for help.

"I don't believe in that crap," I told her.

"That's okay," she replied. "Next time you want a glass of red wine, look up at the sky and say 'Help!' anyway." As anti religion as I was at the time, I followed her advice. And since then I've never had a craving for red wine or any other alcoholic beverage. If only forgiving Leo was that easy.

*Where do we go from here?*

I'm trying to be softer with Leo, more understanding. Even if I'm secretly panicked by the thought of too much clutter littering up the condo, I don't let on. Instead I suggest ways he can save money by shipping his stuff via Greyhound. If someone were to overhear our phone conversations, they'd be impressed by how loving Leo and I are with each other. I just wish I believed it.

# CHAPTER SIXTEEN

## Am I capable of forgiveness?

The day I drove to Phoenix to pick Leo up at the airport, I felt numb. Well, that's not exactly true. I was nervous on the one hand, and relieved on the other. Relieved that this labyrinth of love would finally be unscrambled. Either we'd work it out. Or we wouldn't. The nervousness was different. It had nothing to do with past encounters—when my love addiction would automatically kick in and all was forgiven. I knew that wasn't going to happen. But what if I felt nothing for him? And worse, what if he sensed it?

When I arrived at Terminal 2, Leo wasn't there. I already knew his plane had landed, thanks to the huge screen at Sky Harbor's cell phone parking lot. I also knew he was traveling light so he wouldn't have to hang around the baggage carousel waiting for luggage.

Where could he possibly be?

I watched and waited, fearing an airport cop would wave me away. Fifteen minutes, then half an hour went by. Still no sign of him. Had Leo lost his nerve at the last minute? After I'd been parked curbside for what felt like an eternity, I approached a lady with a cell phone and asked if I might borrow it. I'm probably the only person in the universe who doesn't own a cell phone but I hate them.

I call Leo's cell. No answer.

Explaining my situation to the cell phone lady, she offers to go inside and check on his flight.

"It landed at Terminal 4," she tells me, waving to a man who pulls up beside us. "Good luck!" she whispers before getting in the car and breezing away.

Damn. Why must everything about this relationship be problematic.

I gun the gas pedal and race over to Terminal 4. There

he is, looking lost and forlorn.

"I left a message on your cell," I explain, leaning over and opening the passenger door.

"I figured you'd show up sooner or later."

"I'm so sorry," I say, feeling inexplicably responsible for this latest mix-up.

"They announced the terminal change as we were landing," Leo counters, trying to lessen our mutual discomfort.

"Are you hungry?" I ask.

"Are you?"

"Not really."

Driving back to Sedona, we make careful conversation. He talks about the people sitting next to him on the plane, I fill him in on the latest condo renovations. We act happy to be together again. But it's about as genuine as the smiling plastic elephant on Highway 17, beckoning motorists to come on in and try some of Kid Chilleen's "bad ass ribs."

What I want from Leo is a sincere apology.

He has said he's sorry dozens of times, but I don't feel he means it. It's as if he's parroting what he knows he's supposed to say. And lately he's added an addendum.

"I refuse to be guilted into feeling bad for the rest of my life!"

Intellectually, I understand his point.

Emotionally, I'm not ready to let go of the hurt.

The first few nights we share the same bed, but there's no physical contact. Leo reaches out for me several times and I pretend to be sleeping. After awhile, I use his snoring as an excuse to move to the couch in the living room. Even though he buys anti-snoring medication, I still tell him his uneven breathing keeps me awake.

By the second week, I know it's hopeless.

All my friends accept the fact that I'm a bit neurotic when it comes to clutter. Leo knows it better than anybody, claiming he greatly admires my minimalist philosophy. That's why, before coming to Arizona, he gave away so much of his stuff. Old clothes to the Salvation Army, musical miscellany to his son, camping gear to his daughter. After being in Sedona a few days, Leo wants to drive to Flagstaff to retrieve what's been shipped by Greyhound. Weeks earlier, he had assured me there would only be two guitars and three boxes.

When we arrive at the bus depot and he signs the necessary release papers, there are two guitars and five boxes. "Oh, and by the way, I mailed three more boxes by UPS." To some, this mistruth may seem minor. To me, it simply reiterates the fact that Leo is incapable of being honest.

In every relationship—even ours—there comes a moment truth. That evening, as I was washing up after dinner, I asked Leo if he'd been tempted to drink during the stress of moving.

"Nope," he replies." Not even when I brought a bottle of wine to Mindy's house."

"Mindy?"

"She's a gal in my writer's group who wanted me to read some of her dialog on tape." He pauses, too stupid to realize what a can of worms he's unwittingly opened. "She invited me to dinner last Thursday and I brought a bottle of wine." For a man trying to rebuild trust with me, Leo isn't doing a very good job. "I told you about that, didn't I?"

"I don't think so." A lightning bolt of reality suddenly flashes across my mind. Leo will always be a trickster. Nothing I can do or say will ever change that. I regard him with new eyes, as if I'm seeing him for the very first time. "How would you feel if Hal, my tennis buddy, offered to cook me a meal and I took him a bottle of wine?"

"Not good." Leo sighs, knowing he has screwed up again.

As tired as I am of pointing out his misconduct, I'm sure he's equally tired of trying to live up to my expectations.

"Is she pretty?"

"No," he insists. "No chemistry there at all."

It's my turn to sigh. I don't say it aloud, but my immediate reaction is, "What if there had been?"

Later that day, I meet Hal at a local coffee shop, eager to ask him about his own truthfulness.

"Have you—" I pause, uncertain if I should pursue such a personal line of questioning. "Have you lied a lot in your life?"

"Never."

"Not even a little? "

Hal maintains his parent were old-fashioned in that regard. "They taught us to always tell the truth." He snickers to himself before adding, "In some of my past relationships, honesty hasn't always been the best policy."

I didn't tell him what prompted this latest inquiry, but I'm quite he sensed my unhappiness.

Leo wasn't thrilled about my new male tennis partners, but he kept it to himself. And I made sure I played with the other two guys as much as I rallied with Hal. At one point I did mention my artist friend's exquisite wood sculptures, hinting that an original lamp base made from a piece of juniper or cottonwood might definitely enhance the living room.

"Go for it!" Leo replied, grateful to be able to buy me something.

Picking out which piece of wood might make the best lamp base gave me a legitimate excuse to spend more time in Hal's company. I felt uncomfortable in his house. It was a creaky old place, littered with half finished sculptures, old newspapers and mismatched furniture. He lived there with two other renters who kept changing from month to month. I marveled at his layback attitude—never quite knowing who'd be living there, or if they'd be able to come up with the rent.

I met one roommate. Terry was a toothless, unemployed chef who spent hours and hours writing song lyrics and screenplays. He seemed friendly enough. But Hal told me he had a dark side. In the three months he'd been renting a room, no one had ever phoned or visited the guy. Around rent time, Terry would pay what he could but never the full amount.

"You should be firmer with him," I said.

"Life's too short. Besides, he'll pay me when he can."

I admired how tolerant Hal was.

And, forgiving.

## All in the Family - 1990

Although I've been married twice for real, there was also a third fake marriage. It was the only way I could remain in Canada beyond the nine months allotted visitors. Luckily, I'd met a Canadian man who was eager to marry me. Our wedding was set for October twenty-fifth. My ninety-year-old dad, along with my highly critical sister, were flying to Vancouver to witness this historic event. Neither of them had ever been there and I was looking forward to showing off my newly adopted homeland. But as the wedding date got closer, I began having serious doubts. The groom-to-be was a former school principal and a regular church-goer. But he'd also done time in a medium security prison in Abbottsford (Matsqui) for molesting an Aboriginal boy at his high school. Of course he professed his innocence but I wasn't buying it. Breaking off our engagement, I had exactly fourteen days to find a new Canadian husband.

I told my dad and sister the wedding was off. (I didn't tell them why, of course.) Nevermind, they said. They were coming anyway. To console me. By the time they arrived, I had already married someone else. My sister was staying with an art colleague from UBC and my dad had booked a suite at a nearby hotel. When I told him that I'd already met someone else and wanted them to meet, he scowled.

"I've had it with meeting your men."

"But this one's different."

"I don't care." There was a look of determination in his rheumy old eyes.

"Well, I do," I responded. "You are going to meet Art because he's my new husband!"

My dad was speechless. His first words were very telling. "Does your sister know? "

"No." Clearly, we were both afraid of her reaction and with good reason. When I finally got up the nerve to phone and explain my situation to her, she was livid. First, because it was against the law. Second, because I was being a total hypocrite. I'd recently joined the United Church of Canada which irked my nonbelieving sister no end.

"You claim you're a Christian these days," she said with disgust." Yet you're willing to stand in church and repeat those vows just to get into Canada? "

"You'll get your chance to blast me on Sunday," I answered. "But please be nice to Art at dinner tonight, okay? "

She didn't say another word.

My sister was exceedingly nice to Art, asking him all sorts of computer questions and feigning genuine interest in his answers. My relief was tinged with dread, knowing she and I would be having a no holds barred dinner the next evening.

We met at the Café Alma and, like the dedicated alcoholics we both were, drank ourselves into a state of verbal ferocity. After listening to her lecture me for nearly an hour, I grew weary. When she claimed she was only telling me this for my own good and because she loved me, I lost it.

"You don't love me," I hissed. "What you love is bossing me around. You've been doing it your whole goddamn life! Well the buck stops here. I don't want to hear from you again. Ever. No Christmas cards, no birthday gifts. Not until Daddy dies and we're forced to be civil. You got that? "

She just nodded quietly, picked up her purse and walked out of the café. I was shaking with anger but a few more sips of wine calmed me down. I figured we'd both relent sooner or later.

How wrong I was.

After a year of silence, I started sending her little notes. Cartoons, newspaper clippings. She never replied to any of them. I knew if I phoned, she'd just hang up. So I waited another seven and a half years until our father's death. When I went back east for his funeral she was cool at first, but her hardness eventually softened. No doubt her husband, a psychiatrist, had a lot to do with her change of heart. He must have convinced her to let go of the memory of that horrible fight. I was relieved to have my Big Sissa back and couldn't wait to make up for all the years we'd lost.

Nine months later, at the age of sixty-four, my sister was told she had esophageal cancer. Six months later she was gone. I was devastated. I was also sober by then. After the initial grief passed, I was able to be grateful that we had at least mended the rift between us. If we hadn't, I'm not sure I would've been able to maintain my sobriety.

. . .

Since getting sober fifteen years ago, I've been exposed to a great many AA words that I rejected in my drinking days. *Acceptance* and *Surrender* being two of the most threatening. I've befriended them both now. However, at this stage in my relationship with Leo, I'm less and less able to accept the unacceptable. I remember reading a sentence in one of those how-to-build-a-better-relationship books that I never: forgot" "If you can't see beyond your differences, forget it."

There are so many differences between us. Funny how when you love someone, those differences can be appealing, even sexy. Then, when the love is no longer there, they become huge boulders blocking your path.

Is living with a liar worth it?

To some people, yes. They work out their relationship for the sake of the kids, financial reasons, companionship. When Hal told me he had never lied — even when telling the truth had caused problems — it validated my own belief that without honesty there can be no trust.

In the past when I've said "we're through," it's been in reaction to some wrong Leo has committed. Mostly his lying but sometimes his anger. He acts, I react. But this time I plan to do it calmly. Without fury or impulse.

"But maybe I won't feel the same way tomorrow!" I keep telling myself.

Then tomorrow comes and I'm still unable to wipe the slate clean.

*Am I capable of forgiveness?*

Such a simple thing to do at times. So impossible at others. In my relationship with Leo, I've spent hours, months, even years, excusing, justifying and defending him. I've chided myself for being petty, holding onto to past grievances. One of my sister's favorite expressions was, "I can forgive but I'll never forget!" Back then I thought she was dead wrong, that a big part of forgiveness *is* forgetting. Right now I am incapable of either. That "Lonesome Leo" headline keeps circling around in my subconscious like buzzards over a fresh

kill. What makes it even more maddening is his insistence
that I should simply "suck it up." Love addicts have a gift for
picking impossible partners. Some of us forgive them more
easily than others.

    I just can't. Not this time. Not anymore.

    The person I need to be forgiving is me. So what if my
dreams were unrealistic. So what if my ego kept goading me
into thinking I could make it all better. As Mark Twain once
wrote, "*Forgiveness is the fragrance the violet sheds on the heel that
has crushed it.*" Well I've been stepped on enough. Right now
the only fragrance I'd like to shed on Leo is mace.

# CHAPTER SEVENTEEN

## Should I stay or run away?

Having lived under the same cathedral ceiling for the past ten days without so much as a hug or a kiss between us, Leo still believes everything will work out. "She'll change her mind," he reasons to himself. "She always has before." In the past when we've broken up, I've hated him with a passion. To me, hate is just love turned inside out. This time I don't hate him. I simply don't love him anymore.

A neighbor lady, who is well aware of my current living situation, suggested that I offer to buy him out of the condo. I could even sweeten the deal with a travel bonus. My intuition tells me that if I so much as hint at the idea of a buyout, my arm may get broken again. I don't have the nerve to make such an offer without somebody else being present. We may have only had one physical confrontation in the fifteen years we've known each other, but nothing is written in stone.

Later that morning, I take a mug of coffee into Leo's studio. "I've been thinking about us a lot lately," I say, handing it to him like a peace offering.

"And? " His tone is battle-ready.

"I've made an appointment for us to see a therapist." This isn't what he was expecting me to say. "I don't know her personally," I continue, trying to sound upbeat. "But she comes highly recommended."

"When's the appointment? "

"Thursday. Two o'clock."

"That's your birthday."

"What better present could I give myself? "

"I'm glad we're doing this."

"Me too."

The therapist (I'll call her "Dr. Sue" ) has asked me via email if there's any history of violence in our relationship. I tell her about the broken arm incident and assure her that there's never been a repetition of such aberrant behavior. Before the appointment, I write down exactly how I plan to answer the question I know she'll ask about why we came to see her.

The session takes place in Dr. Sue's home. Her living room is full of earth tones and overlooks Chimney Rock. It's a serene setting except for the two barking dogs that greet us. We remove our shoes while Dr. Sue removes the dogs. I notice Leo has brought along his briefcase. It's filled with our past correspondence, words I'm sure he plans to use against me if it becomes necessary.

Reading from my notes, I begin with, "I'm here to try and end this relationship as amicably as I can." I explain how my partner has attempted unsuccessfully to cheat on me. How this act has destroyed my trust. How, for the past two months, I've tried to repair the emotional damage but still can't seem to forgive him.

I take a deep breath, before dropping the final bomb.

"Leo has invested money in the condo we're presently living in and I'd like to buy him out. I'd pay him his initial investment, plus half the cost of the renovations, plus a five thousand dollar bonus to cover his moving back to Canada."

"Not so fast," Leo replies. The tension in the room is so thick even the dogs outside begin barking. "This was an investment on my part and if you think you're gonna buy me out, you're talking to the wrong guy."

At this point, Dr. Sue jumps in. As luck would have it, her husband is in real estate and she assures Leo that, in this depressed housing market, nothing is going to turn a profit any time soon. Not even in an upscale place like Sedona.

His anger is palpable.

She then asks Leo for his take on our situation. He describes the events that led up to this latest schism between us — his suggestive email to Sonja, how it was an act of self-sabotage that he deeply regrets. He concludes by pointing out that he's never once stepped out on me during our fifteen year relationship.

"What about Lynne? " I remind him, explaining to
Dr. Sue that Lynne was a therapist we'd been seeing before
our third breakup. After we split, Leo paid for a few more
sessions. One included a therapeutic blow job. Lynne later
verified this, begging me to forgive her. I never did. Turning
back to Leo, I remind him of another lady he claimed to have
been intimate with.
          "When you two were a couple? " Dr. Sue asks.
          "No." Leo sounds annoyed.
          "Then what's the problem? "
          "You wouldn't understand."
          Ignoring his adversarial tone, Dr. Sue asks him what he
feels the chances are of us rebuilding our relationship.
          "I'd like to think there's still a chance," Leo replies,
speaking more gently.
          Dr. Sue looks at me, waiting for my response. "There's
not a snowball's chance in hell," I reply.
          Leo immediately gathers up his papers and writes her
a check. As we are about to leave, Dr. Sue encourages us to try
being kind to one another during the difficult days ahead. We
actually manage to have a pleasant birthday dinner that night,
joking and making puns. Then it's back to the condo and our
separate sleeping quarters.

### Give My Regards To Broadway - 1972

          When I was living in Hollywood, RCA Victor offered
me a record contract. Although totally unexpected, I loved
all the publicity and sudden attention. I'd never considered
myself a singer but when "Billboard" and "Record World"
started comparing me to Judy Garland and Eartha Kitt,
I bought into the idea. Eager to begin recording the new
material I'd written for a second album, I was devastated
when RCA didn't renew my contract.
          After the initial disappointment wore off, I suddenly
remembered another of my dad's pet phrases: "One more 'no'
is that much closer to a 'yes!'" If RCA didn't want the material
I'd written for a second album, I'd turn it into a Broadway
musical. "Jesus Christ Superstar" had started out as an album.
Same with The Who's "Tommy."

My album concept was titled "WASP." It revolved around an uptight, New England family with a rebellious daughter. Wonder where that idea came from? I got more hopeful about the project when I met a man (he shall remain nameless) who offered to collaborate on the script. He ran an acting school in Hollywood and had a lot of clout with the New York theater crowd.

He also had a reputation for being difficult.

We began building a story around the songs I had already written. Every Thursday, he'd join me and Joel for a quick bite of Colonel Sanders chicken before delving into the subtext and meaning of every single line of dialog. These suppers became extremely uncomfortable for both me and my Jewish husband. Why? Because all my writing partner ever wanted to talk about were his experiences as a prisoner of war in a German concentration camp.

It took about three months to whip "WASP" into shape. When my coauthor felt it was time to market the musical, he persuaded eight of his acting students to pay their own way to New York City to audition for producers Hal Prince ("Company," "Follies," "A Little Night Music") and David Merrick ("Hello Dolly," "Auntie Mame," "42nd Street").

I couldn't believe this was happening!

As Joel and I boarded the jumbo jet heading for JFK, my writing partner pulled us aside. "I had my lawyer draw up a letter agreement," he told us. "I won't get on this plane until you sign it."

The letter agreement stipulated that no script changes could be made without his permission. It seemed like a reasonable request to me. Frankly, I would have signed my own death warrant at that point.

Next morning—as all of us met with Hal Prince first, then David Merrick—my collaborator decided to read all the parts himself. The eight actors who had shelled out big bucks in order to audition for these Broadway bigwigs sat in stunned silence.

"The script needs work," Hal Prince said at the end of the first audition. "But the score is good. Very original." The second meeting went the same way. David Merrick liked the music but wasn't killed with the book.

My third and last appointment was with a music publisher. The lady in charge of purchasing musical scores gave me an advance of twenty-five thousand dollars. I was in shock. All this had happened as a result of RCA not renewing my contract. Well screw them, I thought. What's a measly record deal compared to a Broadway musical?

I'm not changing a word, my partner later told me. "It's a brilliant script. They don't know what they're talking about."

He was not willing to discuss the matter any further.

Now it was my turn to sit in stunned silence.

The next day, I phoned the music publishing lady and explained the situation. No script changes, no musical. "Give me six months," I pleaded." I'll write another one." Generous woman that she was, she let me keep the advance and waited patiently for me to make good on my promise. It took two years but I wrote another musical. "Rainbow Jones" opened on Broadway at The Music Box Theatre on February 13, 1974.

What did I learn from that experience?

Getting screwed can ultimately turn out to be a blessing. I'm praying that will be the case with Leo. As of now, he refuses to vacate the condo. I can't legally evict him since he isn't a renter. Nor can I slap a restraining order on him. Not unless he gets physically abusive and the cops are called in to settle the dispute. That leaves two options. Either I continue sharing the same space, getting no sleep and feeling more and more defeated by the minute. Or I move out, hoping a solution will present itself later on.

...

The fight or flight response (also called the "acute stress response" ) was first described by Walter Cannon in the 1920s as a theory that animals react to threats with a general discharge of the sympathetic nervous system. With humans, that discharge usually involves a rush of adrenaline, increased heart rate and breathing, constricting blood vessels and tightening muscles. I may not be experiencing any of the physical symptoms associated with the fight or flight response, but I can certainly relate to the psychological ones like anxiety, frustration, anger and fear.

*Should I stay or run away?*

    In the animal kingdom, the weaker lion eventually skulks off into the bush. My runaway response is not like that. Sure, I'm afraid of Leo's brute strength. His ability to wound me with unkind words. But I'm more afraid of staying in this toxic environment, losing whatever grip I may still have on my sanity. I need time alone. Time to nurture and comfort myself. Time to be around people who accept and support me. So much of my self worth has been tied up with Leo's loving me. Well, it isn't anymore.

# CHAPTER EIGHTEEN

## Are we really over?

### TO FRIENDSHIP

We've had our ups. We've had our in betweens.
Too close, sometimes. Sometimes, too far apart.
But lately you have proved what friendship means
By actions made to soothe my sorry heart.
I'd do the same for you were things reversed.
I'd watch your back and try to guide you well.
If you craved help? For sure I'd be there first.
I'd even ride ahead of you to Hell!
Dramatic? (Yes, indeed.) But almost true.
At least that's how you've made me feel this week.
And though my dreams seem blacker now than blue
Such loyalty has brought me to a peak.
Merci, kind sir. May all you've done and said
Bring angels to your ripe and ready bed!

- Jill Williams -

I wrote that sonnet years ago for a friend who was there for me when I really needed one. The same can be said for my friend Ed. When he heard about my situation, he offered to let me use his bedroom while he was living elsewhere.

"You don't have to pay me anything," he said.

Ed was another tennis buddy. A good fifteen years younger than me, he was constantly ogling the ladies hoping to get laid. Soon after he'd purchased his two-bedroom condo here in Sedona, he discovered that living in this sleepy bedroom community just wasn't his cup of tequila. Off he went to Seal Beach, California in search of more skirts.

Meanwhile, he'd rented out his second bedroom to a woman
he'd never even met named Myra. "When I told Myra you'd be moving into my bedroom,
she said it would be nice to have some female company."
According to Ed, she. had recently divorced her pill-popping,
porno-addicted hubby and was still pretty broken up about it.
"You two should have a lot in common!" he added. I agreed
half-heartedly, hoping she wasn't going to bend my ear about
her sad and sorry life. Just as he was about to hang up, he
remembered something else. "Make sure she isn't smoking in
the condo"
        "No problem," I replied, feeling equally turned off
by the idea of dead cigarette butts stinking up the place. Ed
also wanted me to make sure her dog wasn't piddling on the
carpet.
        Funny how some people can be so concerned with a
tenant's messy habits and so oblivious of their own. I realize
Ed wasn't expecting somebody to be living in his bedroom,
especially a neat freak like me. But when I opened the door,
I had to stifle a gasp. Either a cyclone had blown through
here earlier, or Ed was a serious hoarder. The armoire was
overflowing with undershirts, shorts and mismatched socks.
His floor-to-ceiling closet contained crumpled sports jackets,
legal papers and bags of dirty clothes. He'd said I could
move any of his stuff to make room for my own. But where,
I wondered, would I move it when every cubic inch was
already crammed full of crap?
        Still, my gratitude at being able to escape the tension of
living with Leo outweighed any squeamishness I might have
felt. Besides, Ed's bed was incredibly comfortable and there
was a small TV hidden in the closet. "There's a porno flick in the DVD player," he joked.
"You're welcome to watch it!"
        When I entered the bathroom and opened the cabinet
beneath the sink, I stifled a second gasp. There were literally
dozens of half-used toothpaste tubes, packets of rusted razors,
stray Q-tips. Nevermind, I told myself. You've got your
laptop, a throw away cell phone, and lots of new ideas for the
book. Most important of all, you have your privacy.
        After one week of living in such squalor, my

thankfulness began to wear thin. Myra's presence wasn't exactly soothing, either. At times she greeted me with a kind of hyper friendliness. At others, she was just plain rude. I never knew which roommate I'd be approached by. It was exactly like living with my alcoholic mother.

Despite the deplorable condition of my make-do bedroom, the condo complex offered its residents many amenities: two tennis courts, a spacious swimming pool, a hot tub. How I loved soaking in that steamy bubbling water. As each ripple tickled my knees, I felt less threatened by Leo's looming presence.

Of course, Hal was available whenever I wanted company. He worked as an artist-in-residence on Sundays in one of the local galleries and we'd gotten in the habit of going for a bite to eat afterward. I enjoyed experiencing the various plazas with him, seeing through a sculptor's eyes which art pieces spoke to him and which ones didn't.

Shortly after I'd moved in, Myra announced that she was off to Phoenix to visit her son for a few days. This gave me the opportunity to do something I had wanted to do for a very long time.

### The Next Evening

Hal and I are sitting on Ed's patio, sharing stories of his past and mine. Since I've moved out of my previous living situation, he's more willing to discuss his former relationships. Why they fell apart and why the next one won't. Hal knows who he is now. And he doesn't have to prove himself to the rest of the world. He's quite content working with wood, playing tennis, having the occasional dinner with a friend. He's even begun writing an op-ed piece about not cutting music and art programs from high schools because these disciplines are just as vital to a child's development as math and science.

I can tell that my leaving Leo has given Hal hope about our future. The chemistry's always been there. Now we don't have to pretend that it isn't. We move to the couch and begin cuddling with each other. Every once in a while, he pops a succulent strawberry in his mouth. He has inviting lips and a full head of soft, silky hair. I've already asked him if he wants to spend the night, making sure he understands the ground rules: nothing more passionate than a few casual kisses.

During our friendship, Hal has been the consummate gentleman. He's never pried into my private affairs or even made a pass at me. The first to admit he's never been the aggressive type, he also acknowledges that this didn't serve him well in business. It does, however, allay any sexual apprehensions I might have.

Taking my proffered hand, he follows me eagerly into Ed's messy bedroom. We lie beside each other—me in my pajamas, him in his boxer shorts—pretending to watch an old Eddie Murphy comedy special. His fingers linger on my shoulder, tentative and curious. I don't protest or wriggle away. It's as if he's come upon a unique piece of driftwood that he can't resist touching, exploring, caressing. His hand moves closer to my nipple, circling it slowly. I'm getting aroused and so is he. Still, our eyes remain riveted on Eddie hamming it up in his orange leather jumpsuit.

There is an innocence to Hal's seduction. He hasn't been with a woman for three years and it's as if I'm his first one. Knowing these sensual explorations won't go any further than I want them to reduces my fear. I feel freer. So free, in fact, that I actually do climax.

Eddie Murphy's special has long since ended. The TV doesn't matter anymore. We're too wrapped up in each other's touches and tenderness. Hal doesn't guide my hand where I'm sure he'd like it to go. Instead, he shares his gratitude. "Lying next to you is like a miracle. You're so soft and so responsive."

Next morning we wake up, snuggle a little, and then head outside for some early morning tennis. Hal has to be at the gallery by noon and I have other commitments. As we kiss goodbye, there's a look of romantic expectancy in his eyes. I've seen that look in Leo's eyes many times. I can't honestly return it with anything more than an offer of friendship.

I must learn to love myself first.

The cell phone buzzes. It's Ed, calling from California. "I don't know how to tell you this, but I just got a call from Myra and she doesn't want you speaking to her anymore."

"What? "

"I know it's crazy," he apologizes. "But that's what she wants."

"But why? What have I done? "

"Don't ask me."

I'm taken aback. I had deliberately stayed out of Myra's way whenever she was in one of her moods. I'd even offered to walk her yappy little dog. All of a sudden, I understand." She wanted me to babysit her dog and I refused. Is that it? "

"Hey, I'm just the messenger. I don't know what's in that broad's head." Ed chuckles, before adding, "I hear you have a new boyfriend!"

"He's not my boyfriend and who told you that? "

"Honey, nothing in that condo complex goes unnoticed."

Feeling slightly embarrassed that everyone knew Hal had spent the night, I promise Ed not to cause any more trouble. The freedom I've felt being away from Leo is fizzling out fast. Now I'm trapped in the middle of someone else's madness. When I hear the front door open, I pretend I never got Ed's message.

"Welcome back!" I say, cheerful as a daisy. "How was your trip? "

"The twins were little angels," Myra replies, lugging in some boxes and smothering her dog with kisses. "How was your weekend? "

"Terrific." Normally Myra never asks anything about me so this seems like a good omen. Even though the dog has been staying at the next door neighbor's house, I've volunteered to walk her on several occasions. "Roxy really missed you."

"I missed her, too."

Figuring I'd better not push my luck, I hustle into my bedroom. A little past midnight, I wake up with a start. Myra is doing laundry and the machines are right across from my door. I have no idea how long they've been in use, but I can't resist peering sleepily out into the hallway. There she is, mousy brown hair falling in front of vacant eyes, about to stuff another load into the washing machine.

"I realize you just came back from your son's place and probably have a ton of laundry to do, but would you mind. . . maybe. . . doing the rest tomorrow? "

"Don't you ever speak to me again!" she screams.

With that, Myra stomps into her bedroom, slamming the door behind her. The washing cycle continues unabated. As I crawl back into bed, pulling the covers over my ears, I can't help thinking that this situation may turn out to be more stressful than the one I just left.

...

The definition of *triaphilia* is: the tendency to want to hold on to the three connection. Three strikes and you're out? The Trinity? Even joke tellers use the triple-loaded punchline, "A priest, a minister and a rabbi go into a bar." I'm no different when it comes to buying into that old adage about bad things happening in threes. First, I'm forced out of my own home. Second, this psychotic person I'm living with doesn't want me speaking to her. What's next?

Will Ed kick me out?

Will I have to go back and live with Leo again?

Will he destroy my condo out of spite?

(Even I gave three examples.)

*Are we really over?*

Before I moved out, Leo made what I'm sure he felt was a reasonable compromise. He said he would occupy the condo for three months and then leave. I didn't argue. I was too defeated, too defenseless, and too damn tired of trying to be pleasant to a man I could no longer stomach. Ed's offer was such a gift. I was sure I could make it work for me for ninety days.

Leo and I set up a weekly schedule whereby he'd leave at specified times so I could use my computer, pick up my mail, answer phone messages and enjoy the high definition 47" TV I'd paid for. When the resentment would well up in me—like a bad case of indigestion—I'd remind myself, "*It's only for three months.*" I'd look around the living room at my rug murals, the Navajo throw pillows I'd found online, the Southwestern light switch plates. All the little touches I'd created with such love and enthusiasm. How dare he be enjoying this beautiful setting while I'm living in a junk-filled bedroom with a crazy woman and her smelly little dog."

Sometimes Leo would leave notes for me. Mostly about phone messages. The day after I moved out, I drove him to Flagstaff so he could buy a used minivan. A week later, he asked if I knew a good car mechanic. My replies were always civil. But I was careful not to say anything he might construe as pacifying or even appeasing.

Then he made a fatal mistake.

He left me a note, complaining about the TV's poor reception. "If I'm still paying for Direct TV, I expect my money's worth."

That did it.

Here he was, living rent free in my condo. The one I'd paid two-thirds of the money for and renovated all by myself, bitching about my television not working properly. "Use the bedroom TV," I scribbled back.

Funny how something so seemingly unimportant can set the final wheels in motion. I'd been living at Ed's for nearly a month. I wasn't sleeping. I wasn't eating. And I found myself bursting into tears at the most inopportune moments. Hal tried to be helpful but, by then, I was beyond comforting.

About this time another girlfriend came to Sedona on vacation. She took one look at my washed out face, bony arms and lifeless eyes, and said, "You won't last two more months. You need a lawyer."

Three hours later, I'm sitting in the law office of Daniel C. Fitzgerald (a pseudonym). The building bears his name so I figure he has to be a good lawyer. Or maybe his dad was. Dan has prematurely graying hair but he can't be more than mid forties. He has a slight stammer and he strikes me as a congenital nit-picker. As I describe my situation, trying valiantly not to burst into tears, I know beyond a shadow of a doubt that Leo and I are over.

After hearing what I've described, Dan suggests we hand deliver a very non threatening letter to Leo stating the facts. Namely, that I'm willing to pay back his initial investment, plus half the monies we've spent on renovations, plus a travel bonus of five thousand dollar (less the cost of utilities generated while he was living there) provided he leave the condo prior to July 1. The letter would then go on to say, "We recognize that September 1 had been proposed as a deadline for you to vacate the premises. However, the living situation in which my client finds herself has resulted in extreme physical and emotional stress. She needs to get back into the home sooner in order to preserve her health." I knew Dan was wasting his time—and my money—but I acquiesced. We didn't have long to wait for Leo's response. His fax read: "Let's litigate."

# CHAPTER NINETEEN

## What's next?

I'd never been to court before. The fellow I was
involved with after Dee's death, the one who married his
landlady to obtain a work permit, practically lived there. Ray
loved to contest every parking ticket, landlord/tenant dispute,
legal matter he could get his hands on. How I wish he was
here right now. I'd feel a helluva lot more confident with him
in my corner. Alas, my lawyer is nothing like the wisecracking
ones you see on TV courtroom dramas. When I share my
concerns with Hal, he simply shrugs his shoulders, advising
me to "Let the man do his job."

My living situation keeps getting worse. One minute
Myra is weeping on my shoulder, bemoaning the fact that
her ex husband is dating a younger woman. The next, she's
glaring at me, daring me to break the silence.

I don't want to expose Hal to her erratic behavior
so we meet at the art gallery. When we go for coffee, I pay
the bill—claiming it's the least I can do to thank him for his
brilliant editing suggestions. For the past ten months, I've been
working on a book about couples who remarry each other. I
thought the idea had definite commercial potential. Especially,
if Leo and I became one of those couples.

That wasn't going to happen now.

Still, the manuscript I'd written had many fascinating
interviews. I wasn't about to give up on it just because the
ending I had envisioned hadn't panned out. I had signed up
for a writers conference months earlier. It was being held
in Philadelphia six weeks after Leo's final arrival.  I was
of two minds. If we had somehow managed to repair our
relationship, that separation would be good for us. And if
we hadn't? Getting away, even for a few days, would be a
godsend. Either way, I kept telling myself, "By the time you

leave for the conference, you will know whether you and Leo are meant to be together."
I knew the answer to that long before I left.
I also knew that rebounding with Hal wouldn't solve a thing. Yes, his companionship was comforting. The daily phone calls, the occasional coffees. But I didn't love Hal the way he wanted me to love him. The way he deserved to be loved. In the end, it put more pressure on me. What I really needed was a change of scene. Unfamiliar faces, being creatively stimulated. "Your lawyer knows what he's doing," Hal assured me before I took off for Philadelphia. "Stop trying to second guess him and just enjoy the writers' conference."

### The Writers' Conference - 2010

The conference was being held at a Holiday Inn. As I arrived and saw the other attendees, name badges and manuscripts cradled protectively under their arms, I felt like I'd come home. Upon entering my hotel room, soothed by the soft shades of beige and maroon, I couldn't help but whisper aloud, "Free at last!"
The bathroom was equally spotless.
For the first time in weeks, I felt optimistic about my future.
The conference turned out to be everything I had hoped for. I met with several New York literary agents who expressed interest in my book on boomerang lovers. They gave me their business cards and encouraged me to send them a proposal. This was a real boost to my bruised and battered ego.
I had arranged to stay in The City of Brotherly Love" a few extra days, thinking it would give me a better understanding of how this country got started. As it turned out, being away those two days was both a blessing and an adventure. Once the conference ended, I saw no point in paying two hundred dollars a night for my present hotel room. Spending that kind of money for a place to sleep seems ridiculous. Not everyone agrees, of course. Many travelers have difficulty adjusting to a strange bed. Me, I'm more apt to have a sleepless night obsessing over the money I'm wasting

on overpriced accommodations.

I thumb through the local yellow pages and come across a hotel that boasts the incredibly low rate of forty dollars per night. "I'd like to make a reservation," I tell the operator.

"We don't make no reservations, honey."

I pause before inquiring, "How safe is your hotel? "

"Safe as any other place in the city," she replies.

"Well, thank you very much. I may see you later."

"Suit yourself."

A fellow writer I'd befriended at the conference tags along with me and my carry-on to The Caroline Hotel (renamed for reasons that will become obvious later). As he and I take turns rolling my suitcase along the cobblestones, I quickly assess the neighborhood as a safe one. Unless, of course, you happened to be a straight male. The lobby has seen better days. Bags of trash are piled in one corner, cracked linoleum graces the entrance. A desk clerk watches the Phillies beat the Mets on a tiny, sporadically functioning TV. Behind him is a wall of individual boxes for room keys and phone messages. Most are empty.

My companion points out a sign that says: "Anyone who is not a hotel resident will be charged $5 for accompanying hotel residents to their room." Fortunately, asking him to see what's available, the clerk doesn't charge my friend for keeping me company. A wizened janitor, who also serves as the elevator operator, takes us up to the ninth floor. When I ask him how safe the neighborhood is, he echoes what the receptionist has already told me. "Safe as any other place in the city!"

The TV works. The locks on the doors are secure. So what if you have to share a bathroom with a stranger. For forty bucks, it's worth it. Besides, the desk clerk assures me the adjoining room is unoccupied.

The following morning as I try to brush my teeth in the sink, the water doesn't work. Off I go to the nearest Starbucks to make use of their facilities. After people-watching while sipping an Americano, I head out to investigate this historic city. Huge murals painted on numerous buildings immediately grab my attention. So does a deserted carousel, twirling away in the middle of some park. My smile is spontaneous for the first time in weeks. No, months. Time to visit the central library to check my emails. It's an impressive building with polished brass handrails and copper-plated elevators. I'm relieved to find there's nothing from my lawyer. "No news is good news" as far as I'm concerned. But there's no email from Hal, either. We usually correspond on a daily basis.

My second night at The Caroline is far less restful. Getting up to shut off the TV—they don't supply remote control channel changers in this place—I hear two lovebirds really going at it. Screams of passion, the bang-bang-bang of busy bedsprings. Just as suddenly, the moaning stops. I fluff up my rock hard pillow, eager to escape reality and fall asleep.

The moaning begins anew. This time a female voice says, "Hey! Quit that! You're hurting me." He must have quit whatever he was doing because she starts moaning again. More screams of ecstasy, more busy bedsprings. By her third customer, I realize I'm directly above a hooker. A very popular hooker from the sound of it.

I hadn't considered how much these paid professionals enjoy their work.

"Are you kidding," a friend later teased. "The more excited they sound, the quicker the turnover!" I should have figured that out on my own, considering how many times I've done the exact same thing.

Flying back to Arizona, I felt the dread return. Like the clouds outside my airplane window that obscured the earth below, fears about my future overshadowed any positive memories of the writers' conference.

All I could think about was next Monday morning at ten o'clock. Leo had been served with a court date notice. Would his lawyer triumph over mine? And how would I ever get through the next five days?

As a way of distracting myself once I returned to Sedona, I had persuaded a girlfriend to give a dinner party. Hal and another guy I'd met online were invited. I figured an evening of good food, fun conversation and a lively game of "Catch Phrase" would keep me from fixating on something over which I had absolutely no control.

When I entered Ed's condo, something had changed. For one thing, Myra's three vacuum cleaners were no longer cluttering up the living room. And her bedroom door was open. Peering in, I asked, "Is anybody home? " The next door neighbor appeared, her usual smile gone. "While you were away, Myra tried to kill herself."

She'd left a suicide note and, when whatever pills she took hadn't killed her, she went crazy. Destroying furniture and making such a racket that the other tenants became concerned and phoned the police.

"She's in the psych ward in Arizona," the neighbor explained.

Neither of us knew what to say next. So we exchanged phone numbers and she left. I felt sorry for Myra and a little uneasy staying here by myself. The more I thought about her mood swings, her rage at the ex for dating a younger woman, her obsessive clothes-washing, I can't say I was surprised. Maybe that misplaced anger at me had more to do with her plan to commit suicide all along. My presence got in her way.

"How sad and precarious life is," I said aloud, looking at a forgotten dog leash.

As tonight's dinner party approached, the online guy I wanted to fix my friend up with cancelled. What a jerk, giving such short notice. I was also beginning to worry about Hal. Why hadn't he phoned? It wasn't like him to be so loosey-goosey about these things.

Then it came.

An email from Hal's roommate:

PLEASE CONTACT ME BY PHONE AS SOON AS YOU GET THIS MESSAGE. TERRY

"Hal is dead," Terry told me. "I didn't want you to read about it in the paper." Before I could express my disbelief, he continued. "He was bludgeoned to death by our new roommate."

"Oh my god."

"I walked in on them while the guy was still beating on Hal's lifeless body. He was out of his mind and told me, 'You're next!'"

Terry ran out and called 9-1-1. Apparently this new

roomie (found on Craigslist) had decided to stop taking his meds. Part of me didn't believe this was happening.

Wasn't Myra's breakdown enough bad news?

"I just hope Hal died with the first blow," I said, sickened by the idea of anyone being beaten to death with a rock.

"I'm sure he did," Terry replied, hoping against hope that his words were true.

We discussed when Hal's brother would be arriving, where the memorial service was being held. As I hung up, I couldn't help thinking again about how fleeting and precarious life is. I also got scared that Leo might do something crazy.

*What's next?*

After my lawyer advised me, to get out of town for the weekend, I drove to Las Vegas to visit a friend. We both agreed that some stand-up comedy was exactly what I needed. Like creativity, laughter has always been a healthy outlet for me However, this routine didn't lift my spirits one bit:

Comic: Two prisoners are boasting about their crimes. First guy says to the second one, "I robbed a bank and they gave me twenty years. " Other guy says, "I killed a man and I'm getting out in three days." "Three days! How'd you work that one? " "It was a lawyer. "

All I needed to hear was another bad lawyer joke.

Would Monday's court date be a success?

Or would I wind up living in Ed's condo with yet another crazy renter?

On the drive back from Vegas, waiting over five hours at Hoover Dam, I kept repeating The Serenity Prayer. As always, it grounded me and got me feeling grateful.

> *God grant me the Serenity to accept the things I cannot change*
> *Courage to change the things I can*
> *And the wisdom to know the difference.*

# CHAPTER TWENTY

## Who am I now?

### The Courthouse

It's Monday morning. My lawyer and I wait in the parking lot outside the courthouse. I know by the churning in my stomach that Leo will show up. He'll be alone, too. His ego will have convinced him he can be his own best counsel. Within minutes he pulls up in his used minivan, saunters over to my lawyer and hands him a manilla envelope containing two weeks' worth of my mail. I don't acknowledge his presence. Instead, I move behind Dan, all very prim and proper in my tailored black suit.

"All rise!" the clerk declares, as a black-robed judge enters the courtroom. I'm sitting on the right-hand side behind a long narrow desk, going through my mail. We are both sworn in and then, as the Plaintiff, I enter the witness box.

"Are you the sole owner of the property located at—" As my lawyer asks his first and only question, I don't know whether to look at him or the judge. I opt for the latter.

"I am."

Leo and I had agreed that since I was an Arizona resident and I'd invested two-thirds of the money, my name alone should be on title. We could always change it later.

There's an audible snicker from Leo.

Suddenly the judge goes bonkers.

"I do not allow derogatory sounds or utterances in my courtroom. You will have your chance to speak and until then I suggest you keep quiet. Do you understand?"

"I—I do."

As far as I was concerned, I was home free. My lawyer then asked Leo if he had any questions for me. He said he didn't.

Since Leo had no legal counsel, he was told he could remain seated. I knew what was coming next. He may not have the literary brilliance of Ernest Hemingway, but that didn't stop him from thinking he did. And so began a long, rambling history of our relationship. It's beginnings and endings over the years; how I was usually the one to say "It's over" but then I'd relent. He told the judge about his email to Sonja, how badly he felt about it. He also said we'd discussed adding his name to the title. He neglected to mention that he refused to do it until he had paid his half of the initial investment. His final sentence was something to the effect that he was now willing to accept my offer.

My lawyer requested a ten minute recess, hoping we might settle the finances as well as Leo's vacating the property.

"No way," I told him through clenched teeth. "You said yourself that the sole purpose of this hearing was to get him out of my condo."

"Whatever you want."

Maybe I was foolish not to get the whole matter settled in one felled swoop. But it would have required me to speak directly to Leo and possibly haggle with him over a travel bonus that I was now unwilling to pay him. He'd had his chance to leave town six weeks ago.

When the judge reentered the courtroom, he asked my lawyer what statute he was using as an argument since Leo wasn't by definition a renter.

"Forcible detainer, your Honor."

"So moved," the judge said, banging his gavel.

Leo was then asked to pay the court costs, plus half my lawyer's fee. I found it deliciously ironic when he was told to make the check out to me personally. As he was writing it, I whispered to my lawyer, "Give him your card and tell him to contact you. I have every intention of paying him back whatever monies he's invested in the property."

At last it was over, the whole nasty business.

### Down the Road

It's been awhile since I've laid eyes on Leo. He didn't leave town right away. I'd see him at the market occasionally, or the car wash, or driving down Highway 179. At first I was furious with him for lurking in the shadows of my beloved Sedona. It had been my rock filled refuge for the past eight years, not his. I no longer feared running into him the way I used to when we both lived in Vancouver. Back then, Leo was my "drug-of-choice" and I knew — once he spoke to me — I'd be unable to resist him.

It's different now.

If we for some reason came face to face, I'd either ignore him completely. Or I'd nod. No smile, no nervous little wave. The same way I might behave with an auto mechanic who had overcharged me but still fixed my car.

Leo did leave in September as planned. Back he went to Canada and, as far as I know, he's still there. I've had my lawyer contact him since, asking how he wished to be reimbursed. So far, Leo hasn't responded. My sponsor thinks it's his final attempt to control and piss me off. She's probably right, as I detest having unpaid debts hanging over my head.

I've continued seeing Dr. Sue to make sure I don't repeat any self-destructive patterns. One of the characteristics we love addicts have is feeling worthless if we're not in a relationship. I used to minimize that by saying, "Everybody wants to be in a relationship." The fact that I would consistently choose unhealthy ones was something I refused to face.

Another sure sign of love addiction? Serial relationships. I can definitely relate to that. After losing my virginity at age sixteen, I swore to myself that I'd never have more lovers than I could count on one hand. That soon turned into two hands. Then my toes got involved. A girlfriend in college became my official "List Keeper." As long as I could remember their names, I told myself, I wasn't a wanton woman. Besides, I never had sex with any of my serious boyfriends until we'd gone on at least three dates and been to two movies. (I don't consider my Italian captor or the guy I picked up at the voting booth boyfriend material.) Still, like the world's population, those numbers kept increasing. When Leo and I got married, the same college friend sent me the Official List with a note that read, "May your upcoming nuptials end any further need for this!"

Since his departure, a very strange thing has happened. I actually enjoy being alone. In fact, I prefer it to being part of a couple. Is it because, at my age, the partner-choices are much less appealing? Could be. But I think it has more to do with the idea that time is a precious commodity. Wasting any more of it on unfixable relationships just isn't an option.

I've had two "love slips" since Leo and I parted company. The difference is, this time I knew these men were not suitable partners. One had a serious debt problem, the other was a sex addict. In the past, I would've hung in there, trying to either justify their behavior or change it. That's not my concern. Not anymore. And if my mind starts playing tricks on me, Dr. Sue is there to give me a reality check.

### A Chance to Be Better

To quote Albert Camus, "*Freedom is nothing else but a chance to be better.*" Right now, I'm doing the thing that has always given me the most freedom. Being creative. I took Hal's advice to heart—about turning my rug murals into a viable business. Frankly, I get more emotional satisfaction from painting those intricate designs than hunting down another silver fox. That is not to say I don't feel lonely at times. But it passes quickly and I'm back to being me.

Last Christmas Leo and I were, decorating a dinky little tree together. I forget what gifts we exchanged. Or what we did that day. This Christmas, I spent by myself. Painting. Listening to country music. Watching a little TV.

I didn't feel sad.

I wasn't secretly longing for Leo, either.

If anyone had predicted this a year ago, I would have said, "Impossible!"

I have since learned, that nothing is impossible. Life can be fulfilling with or without a man. Or a cat. Or even company over the holidays. Writing this book has taught me so much about who I am, who I was, and, most importantly, why I became a love addict. In the same way that I can't indulge in red wine, I can't afford any ties to Leo. I've had to cut off his son which was a lot harder than I thought it would be. We were very close. And I often wonder if he and his perky little girlfriend ever got married. Guess I'll never know. What I do know is that my spiritual beliefs have helped me to overcome my fears, my love addiction and my uncertainties.

*Who am I now?*

I'm a senior. Female. With a burgeoning career as an artist. I'm single. No kids. Financially secure. Those are the facts. Who else am I? A relatively happy human being. Flawed, of course. Like everyone else. I get a lot of support from friends, my therapy sessions, the Twelve Steps of Alcoholics Anonymous. I am also in relatively good health. I remember when I was in my early teens, asking my dad what he would want if he could have anything in the world. A yacht? A private island of his own? A chorus of long-legged dancing girls?

"My health," he told me.

At the time, I thought his answer was boring.

Now, I couldn't agree more.

# POSTSCRIPT

## Can love addicts recover?

So far, this book has been the story of my boomerang love addiction to the same man. Although we are finally finished, something in me wants others like me, men and women who can't let go of their destructive relationships, to know that they are not alone. More importantly, they don't have to remain in these situations.

First, let's define exactly what a love addict is. I say we have a different DNA than most people. We Do Not Accept (reality, our partner's unhealthy behavior, our own unhealthy behavior, to name a few). Put another way, we're too busy Denying, Negotiating and Appeasing to notice what a dysfunctional mess we've gotten ourselves into.

Although I earned my "Alcohol and Drug Counseling Certificate" from San Bernardino College, I am by no means an expert on the subject of Love Addiction. My knowledge comes from hands-on experience, not book learning. I hope the stories I've shared with you about my unrealistic relationships will shed new light on your own situation. Below are some definitions that may clarify what these terms mean.

### What is love addiction?

Love Addiction usually involves a pattern of frequent relationships that often begin with intense passion and end relatively quickly. A variation of this is the involvement in long-term relationships with dramatic highs and lows, stimulating a similar range of emotions as that found in short-term relationships.

### How do love addicts behave?

Those involved in a pattern of love addiction do not continue such destructive patterns knowingly. It is their absolute belief that the current person is the one that was meant for them, and that they will be together for the rest of their lives—defying all odds and obstacles, if necessary. The meaning that they derive in their own life is directly tied to this belief. In fact, it is this irrational thought process that provides the emotional comfort and stability they seek.

### What is codependency?

Codependency applies to those individuals who willingly sacrifice their goals, their values, and their identity in exchange for the emotional benefits that they gain from playing the salvation role in their partner's life. Without this role, codependents feel that their life would be meaningless. Oblivious to the fact that it is because of these relationships that their lives already are.

### What is boomerang love addiction?

Since I believe I coined that particular term, I'd define it as, "*Someone who keeps going back to the same dysfunctional relationship over and over again, regardless of the consequences.*"

I've asked dozens of boomerang lovers why they've returned to their former (unsuitable) partners or spouses and their justifications include: keeping the family together, finances, sexual compatibility, companionship, religion, even immigration issues.

To help you decide if you are a love addict, here are ten characteristics:

1. Trades sex for love
2. High risk sexual behaviors
3. Meets partner's needs over her own
4. Inability to trust in relationships

5. Intense need to control or please others
6. Relationships make you feel whole
7. Uses relationships to feel high
8. Outer facade of having it all together
9. Serial relationships
10. Feel worthless if not in a relationship

If any of these characteristics describe your behavior regarding relationships, you may want to check out the following websites:

www.slaafws.org/
www.frontrangecounselingcenter.com/women_love_addiction.html
www.thegooddrugsguide.com/addiction-types/behavioral-addiction/relationship-and-obsessive-love-signs-and-treatment.htm
www.allaboutlove.org/love-addiction-recovery-faq.htm
www.recovery-man.com/loveaddict.htm
http://loveaddicts.org/
http://loveaddictionhelp.com/
www.recoverynation.com/
www.ncpg.com/addicted_to_love.php
www.HabitDoc.com

Below are some books on love addiction:

*Facing Love Addiction* by Pia Mellody
*Confusing Love With Obsession: When Being in Love Means Being in Control* by John D. Moore
*Addiction To Love: Overcoming Addiction and Dependency in Relationships* by Susan Peabody
*How to Break Your Addiction to a Person* by Howard Halpern
*The Love Addict In Love Addition* by Jim Hall
*It's All About Love* by Brenda Schaeffer
*Obsessive Love: When It Hurts Too Much to Let Go* by Dr. Susan Forward and Craig Buck
*Take Control Now!* By Dr. Marc F. Kern

*Women Who Love Too Much: When You Keep Wishing and Hoping He'll Change* by Robin Norwood
*Daily meditations for women who love too much* by Robin Norwood

...

*Can love addicts recover?*

## INTERVIEW WITH MARC F. KERN

Today, as a nationally recognized expert in his field, Dr. Kern is known for his compassion, humor and deep understanding of the addictive process. He continues his lifelong study and practice of the newest research-based treatments that will best help his clients with addictions and other destructive, repetitive behaviors. He draws on his own personal and painful experiences with addictions and the life problems that arose from those addictions, including love addiction. Or, as he prefers to define it, "an obsessive preoccupation with another person." The following Q&A may help you decide whether your love relationships are healthy or not—and what to do about it.

Q. Do most love-addicted people have other addictions?
A. In my experience, I would suggest that love-obsessed people have a strong propensity towards other addictions.
Q. With alcoholism or drug abuse, the user must stop using his drug-of-choice. How does that work with a love addiction?
A. Love addiction is a process addiction rather than a chemically-induced one. Like gambling, or shopping, or over-eating. It's akin to an over attachment to someone, an inability to break away in spite of negative or unhealthy consequences. There's usually a sexual component but not always. In some cases, especially with seniors, it's more about sexual fantasies.
Q. How do you help them recover?
A. I encourage them to conceptualize the seductive quality the love object provides.
Q. In other words, the high of infatuation rather than any long term commitment?

A. Exactly. The anticipation is much greater than the reality.
Q. What if they want to keep the high of that anticipation rather than give it up?
A. That's a normal reaction at first. Like some alcoholics, some love addicts have to hit bottom before they seek recovery. Those love obsessed emotions are very enticing.
Q. Assuming they want to recover, what happens next?
A. We begin with the process of disengagement. They have to go through a kind of mourning period. In my own situation, which lasted over two years, the only cure was complete abstinence. From seeing that person, hearing her voice. By doing that, I became proactive in my own recovery process.
Q. What about rebounding into an equally unrealistic relationship with somebody else?
A. I eventually found someone I wasn't madly in love with. I liked her and eventually our bond was more satisfying.
Q. Lots of people would still go for the high over mutual bonding.
A. Lots of people do.
Q. It is said that childhood trauma often makes love addicts out of us. What's your story?
A. I felt love-deprived as a child. I didn't have a mother who was particularly giving on that level.
Q. Would you hazard a guess as to the recovery rate among love addicts?
A. You can mitigate a love addiction, dampen it so it hinders you less in life. But you never completely get over it. I still yearn for that high even though I'm happily married. That yearning is not fully fixable. Like the alcoholic or the addict, they will probably always, on some level, crave their drug-of-choice. There are degrees of love addiction. Some can result in homicides. All of us need to strive for an emotional balance.
Q. Back to the recovery process you use. Can you give more specifics?
A. When the person finally realizes the relationship is not going anywhere, I encourage them to do a personal cost benefit analysis.
Q. Sounds pretty cut-and-dried to me. What kinds of questions do you recommend they ask themselves?
A." What things are you sacrificing to sustain this love? Is

the relationship the central focus of your life, the main reason you feel good about yourself? Does it impede you from more healthy, adaptive behaviors like exercise, being available to family and friends?

Q. Would you care to add anything else?

A. You asked me earlier to define process. It's a ritual, meaning it's acquired. Even if these processes are not chemically-induced, a person over time can self-create a chemical imbalance.

. . .

I'd like to encourage anyone who is currently in a love-addicted relationship — whether it be a new one, or a repeat performance — to answer the questions I've asked myself throughout this book. Some of them may not apply in your case. But some of them might. Your answers may clarify why you keep doing the same thing, expecting a different result. Conversely, they could prove that this one last time was worth it. Either way, I wish you luck!

## CHECKLIST

1. Why go back again?
2. Is being alone that bad?
3. What are my expectations?
4. How important is sex?
5. Will money be an issue?
6. What about family and friends?
7. Why is our relationship different this time?
8. Am I being realistic?
9. Who was I growing up?
10. Which parent am I trying to replicate?
11. Are old patterns resurfacing?
12. Is a new project the answer?
13. Why do I still have doubts?
14. What happens now?
15. Where do we go from here?
16. Am I capable of forgiveness?
17. Should I stay or run away?

18. Are we really over?
19. What's next?
20. Who am I now?

CPSIA information can be obtained at www.ICGtesting.com
Printed in the USA
270303BV00006BA/9/P